FRANKENSTEIN
A play
by
John L. Balderston
&
Garrett Fort
1931

Books by
Philip J Riley

CLASSIC HORROR FILMS
Frankenstein, the original 1931 shooting script
Bride of Frankenstein, the original 1935 shooting script
Son of Frankenstein, the original 1939 shooting script
Ghost of Frankenstein, the original 1942 shooting script
Frankenstein Meets the Wolfman, the original 1943 shooting script
House of Frankenstein, the original 1944 shooting script
The Mummy, the original 1932 shooting script
The Mummy's Curse the original 1944 shooting script (as Editor in Chief)
The Wolfman, the original 1941 shooting script
Dracula, the original 1931 shooting script
House of Dracula, the original 1945 shooting script

CLASSIC COMEDY FILMS
Abbott & Costello Meet Frankenstein, the original 1948 shooting script

CLASSIC SCIENCE FICTION
This Island Earth, the original 1955 shooting script
The Creature from the Black Lagoon, the original 1953 shooting script (editor-in-chief)

THE ACKERMAN ARCHIVES SERIES - LOST FILMS
The Reconstruction of London After Midnight, the original 1927 shooting script
The Reconstruction of A Blind Bargain, the original 1922 shooting script
The Reconstruction of The Hunchback of Notre Dame, the original 1923 shooting script

CLASSIC SILENT FILMS
The Reconstruction of The Phantom of the Opera, the original 1925 shooting script

FILMONSTER SERIES - LOST SCRIPTS
James Whale's Dracula's Daughter, 1934
Cagliostro, The King of the Dead, 1932
Wolfman vs Dracula 1944
Lon Chaney as Dracula/Nosferatu
Robert Florey's Frankenstein 1931
Frankenstein, A play - 1931

AS EDITOR
Countess Dracula by Carroll Borland
My Hollywood, when both of us were young by Patsy Ruth Miller
Mr. Technicolor - Herbert Kalmus
Famous Monster of Filmland #2 by Forrest J Ackerman

FILM DOCUMENTARIES
A Thousand Faces - as contributor (Photoplay Productions)
Universal Horrors - as contributor (Photoplay Productions)

Mr. Riley has also contributed to 12 film related books by various authors
as well as numerous magazine articles and received the Count Dracula Society Award
and was inducted into Universal's Horror Hall of Fame

Hamilton Deane as Frankenstein with Dora Mary Patrick from the Little Theatre Production of the play of Peggy Webling's play

Hamilton Deane as "Frankenstein."—All photos courtesy of Ivan Butler, who portrayed Victor in this original stage production of 1930

Published by:
BearManor Media
P O Box 71426
Albany, GA 31708
Phone: 760-709-9696
Fax: 814-690-1559
books@benohmart.com

©2010 Philip J Riley
For Copyright purposes
Philip J Riley is the author in the form of this book

We present this script for historic reaseach only. Actual production of this play may require permissions
Script by John L Balderston and Garret E. Fort, 1931
Cover Art - ©2010 By Philip J Riley - Since none of the scripts in this series
were thought to exist and were never produced, we have created mock-up posters in the vintage style of the period.

Cover art by Paul Spatola

The Author would like to thank the following individuals who contributed and helped make this series possible. Carl Laemmle Jr., R.C.Sherriff, Stanley Bergerman, Gloria Holden, Jane Wyatt, Otto Kruger, Marcel Delgado, Robert Florey, Paul Ivano (Cinematographer), Paul Malvern (producer), Elsa Lanchester, Merion C Cooper, Patric Leroux, Bette Davis, Bela G. Lugosi, Sara Karloff, Technicolor Corporation, John Balderston III, Douglas Norwine, Loeb and Loeb Attorneys, David Stanley Horsley, Bernard Schubert, John Teehan, Gregory Wm. Mank, George Turner, Ernest B. Goodman, Universal Legal Department, Ivan Butler.

Author's Note: I interviewed the producers, directors, stars, cast and crew in the early to late 1970s. They were recalling events that happened 35-45 years previous and sometimes memory fades or events are recalled from their perspective point of view.

First Edition
10 9 8 7 6 5 4 3 2 1

The purpose of this series is the preservation of the art of writing for the screen. Rare books have long been a source of enjoyment and an investment for the serious collector, and even in limited editions there are thousands printed. Scripts, however, numbered only 50 at the most. In the history of American Literature, the screenwriter was being lost in time. It is my hope that my efforts bring about a renewed history and preservation of a great American Literary form, The Screenplay, by preserving them for study by future generations.

Recommended reading - Hideous Progenies: Dramatizations of Frankenstein from
Mary Shelley to the present by Steven Earl Forry,
University of Pennsylvania Press, 1990

Frankenstein

by
John Balderston
&
Garrett Fort
A play in Three Acts

(Presented by Philip J Riley)

Hollywood Publishing Archives

In 1931 John L. Balderston was hoping to repeat his huge success with the American play version of Dracula. Before production started on the 1931 Universal film version he wrote a play of "Frankenstein" with screenwriter Garrett Fort. Although it was never produced it is still an important document in American Theater history. It is here, in this play, that we discover how the name Frankenstein was attributed to the monster instead if his maker. I'll have to reread the Peggy Webling play to see if the same occured in the Hamilton Deane London production. This volume is a companion piece to Robert Florey's "FRANKENSTEIN book also published by BearManor Media and was written a month earlier in 1931

Editor

FRAKKENSTEIN

```
    *
   ***
  *****
   ***
    *
```

By
The Authors
of
DRACULA

(Copies
April 10, 1931)

ACT I 1-1

SCENE: The combined study and laboratory of Henry Frankenstein, in an old house at Goldstadt. Door R.F. leads to kitchen, and R. leads to bedroom. Beyond this, a deep recessed window now with the curtains drawn, and with a tall screen folded and propped against them. Along the back wall is a rough work table, and shelves above, all a litter of bottles, retorts, pestles and mortars, burners and other paraphernalia of a laboratory. A skull on one of the shelves, the bones of a hand on another.

There is also a door in this wall leading into the garden, and across the corner, a large cupboard. The whole wall L. is covered with untidy book-crammed shelves except for the fireplace in the centre, with mirror above. The firelights show Henry's writing table, piled with large books, some of them open, and a lamp. Some chairs near. No other furniture in the conventional sense, but before the recess, a tall, intricate machine of cords, batteries, metal discs and such, and either a low table or a tall bed, shrouded with a cloth. These are dimly seen by the flickering light of one candle on the work table, and one on the floor.

There is a thunderstorm outside.

AT RISE: HENRY FRANKENSTEIN is crouched on the floor, working at machine, back to audience, silhouetted by candle. There are some hisses and sparks. FRITZ, crouched in the fireplace uses the bellows and in the sudden glow can be plainly seen. He looks like a gnome, with a thin child's body and an old man's face.

HENRY

Now I have it!
    (machine hisses, sparks, sudden light
    and darkness)
Oh, good God, it's gone again. Fritz, bring me that lead.
    (FRITZ carries him a small heavy pot
    from the ashes of the fire. They crouch
    together at the machine, working, two
    silhouettes)

HENRY (continued)
There. that will hold.
>   (Pulls out two metal discs attached
>   to machine, lays them at head and foot
>   of table)

Poor Fritz are you tired? But it can't be helped. We must work while the storm rages, you know.
>   (FRITZ nods)

We've not had such a magnificent one for two months. Do you remember it?
>   (FRITZ makes a gesture of terror)

It wasn't pleasant, was it, up there in the woods? Hand me that rope.
>   (He works away, more lightening and thunder
>   outside)

Good, it's coming nearer. I'll connect this and see what we get.
>   (Goes back of machine, comes out,
>   waits - lightning outside and
>   instantly, a blue spark shoots
>   from one disc to another inside
>   the machine)

My God, that's what I want
>   (Thunder, FRITZ recoils in terror)

Fool! You're afraid of the noise.
>   (He has disconnected something behind
>   the machine while talking)

It's the spark you should fear! Fritz, I must find out how to store up this heavenly fury, this divine wrath that is being poured down on us. I will --- after tonight.
>   (Goes to table and fuses with
>   bottles and tubes)

Come on Fritz, we must work. There may not be another storm like this for months. Tonight!
>   (He is working up to a great state of
>   excitement - pouring, measuring,
>   holding tubes and bottles to the
>   light. FRITZ pulls the table partly
>   out of the recess, begins adjusting
>   one metal plate to one end.

Tonight, if the storm lasts, if my liquid turns - - - -
>   (Flings down and breaks a small bottle)

Wrong! Again! It can't be wrong -- the storm may pass --
>   (Rushes to large book on table,
>   turns pages, studies excitedly
>   holding one bottle in his hand)

It can't be - I did this - and this -
>   (Mutters over book, FRITZ creeping
>   up to look over his shoulder.
>   Shouts suddenly.

Of course, of course! I've got it now, I've got it!
>   (Back to table, business with bottles
>   again, FRITZ helping, finally pours
>   fluid into two small vials)

Now, get the machine ready - we'll wait, then on the next big flash - - -
>   (Knocking on door off stage R.
>   FRITZ jumps up, gesturing excitedly)

HENRY (CONTINUED)
Good God, who would come out on a night like this! Don't
answer it, Fritz, they'll think I'm asleep.
>   (Louder knocking)

Nobody knows, what I'm doing but you, and you can't talk!
>   (Knocking, which suddenly stops)

They'll come into the garden and back here. Be quick, the
screen
>   (They push back the table, pull the
>   screen around it, partially hiding
>   the machine also)

I hear someone - Hell and Damnation! Fritz, I'll go into
my bedroom. Tell whoever it is, I am not here - - don't let
anyone in. Say I - - I forgot. Well, write it then.
>   (Blows out candles - goes into bedroom.
>   (Knocking on other door. FRITZ stands
>   in a comic indecision, and at the second
>   knock, opens the door slowly. Rain
>   and wind outside, and two figures with
>   the lightning back of them.

WALDMAN'S VOICE
Is Mr. Frankenstein at home?
>   (FRITZ shakes his head, attempts to
>   bar door)

Henry! Henry! are you in?
>   (Very gently Fritz is pushed aside
>   and DR. WALDMAN enters, followed
>   by VICTOR, both wearing dripping
>   wet cloaks. DR. WALDMAN, priest's
>   costume, a gentle scholarly man.
>   VICTOR is young, with good looks
>   and a boyish charm)

Surely, Fritz, you'd not keep us out on a night like this?
>   (They go to fire. Remove cloaks)

VICTOR
>   (To Waldman)

He must be here. He's not at the inn, nor with any of his
old friends.

WALDMAN
I'm sure he's here. Fritz, my lad, go to your master's room
and see if he is asleep. If he is, don't wake him, but come
back here. If he is awake, write my name - Dr. Waldman and -
a friend.

VICTOR
Oh, he can give my name. Tell him Victor Moritz.
>   (As FRITZ stands silent)

Didn't you hear - - say Victor Moritz.
>   (FRITZ makes a gesture of helplessness)

What's the matter with him, Dr. Waldman, is he deaf?

DR. WALDMAN
No, he can hear, but he can't talk. Go on Fritz.

>   (As the boy exits R. reluctantly)

VICTOR
Who's he?

WALDMAN
The son of a herdsman, up on the Weissenberg. He was born with only part of a tongue, he's never been able to speak.

VICTOR
How ghastly! What strange freaks there are among the mountain folk. How long has Henry had him?

WALDMAN
Eight months, perhaps. He found him - oh, a few months after you went away. He's taught him to read and write a little.

VICTOR
(Examining bottles, etc.)
He's made his study into a laboratory since I left.

WALDMAN
Ah, he has been doing brilliant work in anatomy, galvanism, chemistry of the tissues -

VICTOR
This is like a corner of some ancient shop. Gruesome, these.
(Pointing to skull, etc.)
Look! Here's a book on alchemy - he was always reading them even when he was a boy. He wanted to find the philosopher's stone, or turn base metal into gold, in those days.

WALDMAN
He has deserted his alchemy for the new scientific truths. They fascinate me, as a man of science, though sometimes they terrify me as a priest.

VICTOR
(Laughs)
Don't you find it hard to be both, Doctor?

WALDMAN
I am hoping science will be only another way of proving God, my son.

VICTOR
(Feeling rebuked, begins wandering around the room)
Why doesn't he come, or why doesn't that boy return?

WALDMAN
I hope he is not ill in there. I haven't seen him at one of my lectures in weeks.

VICTOR
Strange! He depended on you so.

WALDMAN

Not any longer. I can teach him nothing. He knows far more than I, or any of his professors.

VICTOR

He is the glory of our University. I know. I heard about him as far away as Paris.

WALDMAN

Is that irony, Victor? Do you still feel bitter?

VICTOR

No Father, not any more. Haven't I brought you out, on the worst night in months, because I wanted to apologize to him?
       (He wanders over to the machine, looks
        at hit)

WALDMAN

I warned you you'll find him changed -

VICTOR

You said he was nervous, high-strung, from over-work. He was always nervous. What's this machine?

WALDMAN

I do not know. I've not been here for -

      (Door burst open. Enter HENRY, followed
       later by FRITZ)

HENRY

Victor! Dr. Waldman! Why have you come here!

VICTOR

Henry!

HENRY

Come away from that machine!

WALDMAN
      (gently)

My son!

HENRY
      (Quieter)

My apologies, father. But the machine must not be touched. Victor, forgive me. I'm a fool. I've got spy-mania. I've been afraid of people prying about trying to find out things. So forgive me.

VICTOR

That's all right. Henry. Indeed, I came to beg your forgiveness.

HENRY

Mine? Why?

VICTOR
(Jerkily, he finds this a little
difficult)
Our quarrel - last year - was my fault. Amelia - preferred you to me. She loved you more than me. It was childish of me to quarrel about it. So I beg you to - - -

HENRY
(Touched by this)
Please don't say it, Victor. The fault was mine. I should not have let her see I loved her. I did not know you cared so much until after you had gone.

VICTOR
It was an engagement from childhood. She may well have been bored with me. And you, with your brilliance, have more to offer her.

HENRY
(Holds out hand)
Friends?

VICTOR
Friends!
(They clasp hands. WALDMAN comes and lays a hand on each shoulder)

WALDMAN
This is better. Now I am happy also, my sons. Now everything will be as it was before.

HENRY
I have not welcomed you back yet, nor asked about your travels.

VICTOR
A scholar's journey. The universities of Vienna, Padus, Rome, Paris.

WALDMAN
A romantic coute. I want to hear more, Victor.

VICTOR
I want to tell you everything. But Henry, were you asleep, when we came? Have you been ill?

HENRY
(Nervous at once)
Ill? No. Who told you that?

VICTOR
No one. But they are worried about you at home.

HENRY
How do you know? Have you been at Belrive?

VICTOR
No, I am going there tomorrow. I came directly back to
Goldstadt from Vienna. But I found letters at the inn.
                (WALDMAN has gone to the table, and
                is looking at one of the old books)
One from your mother, asking me to write her about you.
One from your sister, saying you had not been back there
for five months.

HENRY
        (Evasive)
I have been working - hard. Doctor, I ask your pardon. I
have not even offered you a chair.

WALDMAN
No matter, Henry. I am much interested in this old book.
A treatise in BLACK Letter, on anatomy, with curious draw-
ings by a pupil of Albrecht Durer.

HENRY
        (Enthusiastic at once_
The old anatomists lack our knowledge of detail, tut they
glimpsed intuitively some truths that you men of today don't
understand, Dr. Waldman. You stress detail...detail...
always detail, but you don't see the wood for the trees.

WALDMAN
        (Humorously)
No doubt, no doubt.

VICTOR
Are you going to give a lecture to Dr. Waldman, Henry?

HENRY

Why not?

VICTOR
My dear friend, what IS the matter with you tonight?

HENRY
Nothing, nothing. Sit down, I want to talk to you.

VICTOR
First you want to keep us out and now you want to talk to us,
                (Sits down by Waldman. WALDMAN, placid
                and calm, lights a pipe. HENRY walks
                about)

WALDMAN
        (Lightly)
I can see nothing but a black shape pacing about in the
shadows, Henry. Does this communication of yours require
mystery and firelight?
        (Lightning and thunder)
With an appropriate accompaniment from the elements?

(WALDMAN turns up lamp on table so that
his face and VICTOR'S are illuminated.
During following scene, as HENRY reaches
his climaxes he sits at table, peering
into their faces, his own lit up, then
gets up and walks about again)

WALDMAN (continued)

Henry Frankenstein, may I say something first? You have been
working too hard, and when a MASTER says that to his PUPIL,
you may be sure there's something in it.

HENRY

Tonight, it is you who are to be the pupil, and I the master.

VICTOR
(Shocked)

Really, Henry! Look here - -

WALDMAN makes a pacifying gesture to
Victor)

VICTOR

Dr. Waldman is right. Look at yourself in a mirror. They're
worried about you at home. Ride back with me, if only for a
few weeks.

WALDMAN

Belrive is less than a day's ride across the mountains to
the lake isn't it? Go back with Victor tomorrow.

HENRY
(Paces around impatiently)

How can I go home, when I've so much to do here?

(Thunder again)

VICTOR

I also had a letter from Amelia.

HENRY
(stops suddenly, in an acid tone of
voice)

Complaining of my neglect?

VICTOR

Naturally not. But she said she hadn't heard from you for
months, and obviously she was worried.

HENRY
(Explosively)

She can wait!

VICTOR
(Angry - on his feet)

Henry, you can't talk like that about Amelia to me! Did
you take her away from me simply to break her - - -

HENRY
Did you come up here tonight to be friends, or to tell me
my duty towards my family and my betrothed?

WALDMAN
Gently, my children.

HENRY
(more quietly)
Believe me I love her faithfully, Victor. I shall make her
proud of me. It is because of her that I have worked so
hard on - on this new experiment. Dr. Waldman, it's true
I meant to keep you out, but now I want to talk to you.

WALDMAN
Go on Henry. Victor, come sit here by me.

HENRY
I'm glad you came though I was going to go through with this
alone, that is, with only Fritz. But you are my oldest and
dearest friends! It was Victor who listened to my first
childish speculation about science, it is you, Dr. Waldman,
who have been my confessor, adviser, my teacher ---
(Thunder. It distracts his attention)
No matter. I must hurry. I can only do this with the storm,
and that may be over in a quarter hour.

VICTOR
With the storm? I don't understand.

HENRY
Wait! I must explain something first. Dr. Waldman, do you
remember what we talked about when you came and dined with
me here?

WALDMAN
That was about two months ago. I remember we sat up half
the night and that we talked a great deal of nonsense.

VICTOR
I can't imagine you talking nonsense, Dr. Waldman.

HENRY
What sort of nonsense was it?

WALDMAN
We were discussing the mystery of life, the physical processes
of decay after death, even the nature of the vital force
that infuses life into inanimate matter.

HENRY
(To Victor)
We had been working that afternoon with a toad, killed by
the shock from a galvanic battery. The heart no longer
beats, but the electric current makes the limbs move and
there is a semblance of life.

WALDMAN

A fantastic semblance of life. But as you say, the heart no longer beats, the creature is dead. It is merely muscular contraction.

HENRY

Does a beating heart necessarily signify life? I had a heart that very evening, in a jar in that cupboard steadily beating, Doctor --- was it dead or alive? I killed a dog to steal its heart.

VICTOR

Good heavens, But - why -

HENRY

It had been beating for days. I kept it in a fluid that stopped decay, with a current of electricity passing through it. It pumped that fluid in and out steadily --- until I threw it away.

WALDMAN

But why didn't you show it to me?

HENRY

I meant to. But you said you were afraid our talk had been foolish and perhaps a little wicked.

VICTOR

Wicked? Why wicked?

WALDMAN

Because, my son, it is not for a priest, still less is it for a layman, to probe these things too deeply. We know that life comes from God, from God alone. It is presumption to think the human mind was ever intended to fathom these supreme mysteries -

HENRY

On the contrary, it is cowardice that prevents us from solving them.

WALDMAN

It is presumption, Henry, for us who study anatomy, even for you to whom God has given genius, to push enquiries so far. We must remember that we can deal only with matter, not with spirit, which is the breath of God.

HENRY

Yet you discussed enthusiastically with me, the possibility of destroying life and creating it again.

VICTOR

You are nothing if not ambitious, Henry

WALDMAN

It was only foolish speculation. I was not serious.

HENRY

For weeks I had worked on that problem of the heart. If it could be made to pump a fluid in and out of itself, why would it not be made to pump blood, real, warm living blood? I began gradually draining off the fluid and feeding it blood -- no matter, I must hurry with my story. After our talk, I made a discovery. I have killed toads, and cats and dogs -- killed them, you understand, and now they are alive, in my garden.

WALDMAN

That is not possible, they only seemed to be dead.

HENRY

The WERE dead.

WALDMAN

(Uneasily)

I do not think the Church would approve of these experiments. There is an error - somewhere.

HENRY

There is no error. One was dead 14 hours - their hearts ceased to beat - now they are alive.

VICTOR

(Awestruck)

Wonderful, Henry. So that's what all this mystery has been.

HENRY

Does the man of science, Doctor, ever stop when in pursuit of the truth? I did not stop there.

VICTOR

You don't mean --

WALDMAN

(on his feet)

Your studies have been too much for you. I shall bring a doctor to see you.

HENRY

Sit down and listen. You must listen! You are here tonight to share with me my hour of triumph, or to condole with me in my defeat. Between the bodies of toads and dogs and the bodies of man, what is the difference? Are we not all animals?

WALDMAN

You speak like a heretic. Man is not an animal!

(Sternly)

Go on.

HENRY

After animals, MEN!

(Both men are up, horrified)

VICTOR

Henry, you don't mean you've ... Oh, forgive me.

HENRY

I am no murderer.

WALDMAN

Then what are you trying to tell us?

HENRY

(Almost unheeding them, as thought to
himself, as he paces in the shadows)

My task has been horrible, horrible. I have profaned the resting places of the newly-dead. With my own hands I have dragged bodies to my workshop, with only the help of this terror-stricken lad.

WALDMAN

(Horrified)

What impious perversion of science is this? You have desecrated sacred ground...

VICTOR

If you were trying to bring the dead to life, we'll keep your secret about the bodies. But of course now we must get you away from here ....

WALDMAN

And you must seek absolution and penance from The Holy Church.

HENRY

Dr. Waldman, I will let you remain here, not as a priest, but as a master of science.

WALDMAN

(Drosses R. points to screen)

Henry Frankenstein, what have you behind that?

VICTOR

(as HENRY staggers to table, half
collapses)

What is it, Henry. You are ill --

                    HENRY
No, not ill, only tired. I mustn't be tired, I must have
the courage of the devil, tonight. Fritz -

          (FRITZ jumps up from his corner
          of the fireplace)

Get me that bottle on the shelf, pour me out a drink.

          (FRITZ opens cupboard door, as it swings
          out, it shows a full length, rattling
          skeleton hanging to a peg driven into
          the door. VICTOR, turning around jumps
          back in horror. HENRY swallows drink
          at a gulp, revives enough to laugh,
          mockingly, at Victor's fright)

The skeleton in my cupboard, Victor! He's become an old
friend of Fritz. Did you never meet him?

          (Pushes back hair. Settled quietly
          at table, WALDMAN takes bottle
          sniffs it and looks worried. FRITZ
          puts things away and resumes seat
          by fire)

Ah, now I'm better!

          (They settle at table)

Those who died of disease, whose life machine had already
run down like a worn out clock, defeated me. Corruption
set in too soon. So I failed.

                    WALDMAN
Ah!

                    HENRY
I turned to violent death for my experiments.

                    WALDMAN
          (Horrified)
That thief, who was hanged in chains on the gibbet above
Goldstadt!

          (Accusingly)

The body disappeared!

                    HENRY

It took me four hours to knock off the chains; Fritz and
I could scarcely drag the corpse up here before daylight.

VICTOR

But you failed.

HENRY

Yes, strangulation defeated me. When the spinal cord is snapped, and the chain of nerves that connects the brain and the body is broken, I can do nothing. I could get a heart re-action - that was encouraging, it showed I was on the right track. But the experiment was of no more interest than the beating heart in the jar.

VICTOR

So then - -

HENRY

Then - - Dr. Waldman, do you remember the great storm from the Jura mountains, that swept down the valley - - - -

WALDMAN

Six weeks ago. The lightning play all night.

HENRY

In the village of Pontoise, that night, a house was struck and a man killed - a young man, Doctor, healthy and strong! Dr. Waldman, what was that death, but the same shock from a galvanic battery with which I kill a frog, or a dog?

WALDMAN

(Sternly)

You desecrated that man's grave?

HENRY

I took my implements, my batteries with me and I took Fritz. It took us two days. We hid the body in the woods when it grew light, and went back again at twilight the next night. There was another storm - I brought him to life, there in the forest.

WALDMAN

Impious! A century ago the Church would have burned you - - -

HENRY

Is he who saves a dying man impious? This young man was dead. If I could give him life, would men regard me as a criminal, or as a saviour.

WALDMAN

The doctor does not interfere with the will of Heaven. Henry Frankenstein. He restores the sick BEFORE their souls have gone to God, not afterwards.

                    VICTOR

Your studies have been too much for you, Henry. I will
help you rebury the corpse.

                    HENRY

You need not bother - we reburied it afterwards.

          (The men are terrified)

Why are you so horrified, now, Dr. Waldman? I merely
let his life run out. I was simply not interfering with
the will of Heaven.

          (They remain speechless. DR. WALDMAN
          crosses himself)

I was not interested in his soul, that was n concern
of mine. Nor his body, once I had made it breathe. For
what was all that but my old experiment with frogs and
dogs?

          (Rising to a violent pitch)

I did not want to RESTORE, I wanted to CREATE life.

          (Goes toward machine. Lightning
          and thunder)

                    WALDMAN
          (Weakly)

Create?

                    HENRY

Create! From the beginning.

          (Voice goes flat but gradually rises
          toward end of speech)

I had found ways of slowing up corruption but I had to
work fast. I know my way about the graveyard. I stole
the key of your dissecting room - I took what I needed
as I dared - a bone or a lung or some complicated nerve
tissue. I am a sculptor; I moulded a figure, and a face.

(To Dr. Waldman)
Do you remember then days ago when you were dissecting a brain?
It disappeared; some of it. I was the thief! From charnel
house and burying ground, I fashioned a body -- I made a man!
I have created ---

WALDMAN

A patched up, loathesome Thing, perhaps - but not life.

HENRY

Tonight we'll see. Victor, will you come with me?
(Smiles down on him ironically)
Are you afraid to come. Then Fritz shall help.

(At his name. FRITZ gets up, begins to
push back screen. VICTOR, decidedly un-
willing by this time, stand by machine)

VICTOR

Is this part of it?

HENRY

Part of it -- listen!

(Sudden enthusiasm)
Dr. Waldman -- for the benefit of any unscientific friend here
-- what is the highest color in the spectrum, the last color
we can see?

VICTOR

(Annoyed)
Violet. I know that, at least.

HENRY

Ah! But beyond that - we cannot see it -- is another, stronger
violet -- an ultra-violet. It is -- hotter than sunlight, yet
part of it. It is the life inside the sunlight.

VICTOR

A color you cannot see.

HENRY

Call it another name then - call it a ray, anything. Call it
magic, for it seems like magic. It gives strength, it heals,
it rebuilds. There is health and well-being in that ray. But
that is for the future to work out. While I was thinking of
that, I remembered how you and I used to play on the shore of
our lake at Belrive, and how we watched queer forms of life
created in pools of muddy water, warmed by the sun.

VICTOR

Snails, slugs, not even insects.

                    HENRY
But they moved, they crawled - life, Victor, stirring there,
under our noses.

                    VICTOR
Well - - -

                    HENRY
Already I had found one color, one ray, beyond the spectrum.
          (Violently)
I went beyond that. I found another ray, hotter than Ultra-
violet, of more powerful magic, life-giving, even life-creating!
in the beginning of the world, of all things - - -

                    WALDMAN
          (Loudly)
In the beginning was the Word and the Word was God.

                    HENRY
The word - - the will to create. And God - - perhaps He is a
Ray, and unseen Ray far beyond the visible spectrum!

                    WALDMAN
Blasphemer!

                    HENRY
Why? You too have seen the *sun bring primitive forms of life
out of nothingness - insects from puddles, more complex,
crawling creatures from a bed of warm slime. You catch the
sun in a prism and break it into the seven colors of the
spectrum, and think you have finished with it! I tell you that
beyond your eyesight there exists - - -

                    WALDMAN
You have discovered some new force - - -

                    HENRY
I have! In this machine, there are all the rays of the spectrum,
the ultra-violet, beyond that - - - and beyond that, the Great
Ray which in the beginning brought life into the world, as its
hot mass cooled.

          (Gesture)
But you would not understand.

                    WALDMAN
I understand now what you are trying to do, and in the name
of Religion I forbid it!

                    HENRY
In the name of Science - - remain and verify it!

                    WALDMAN
            (sternly)
Wait! Do you believe in the after life, in the soul?

                    HENRY
I am no atheist.

                    WALDMAN
Then answer me, when this man in the mountains died, was not
his immortal soul summon to Heaven, to Hell, or to Purgatory?

                    HENRY
            (Impatiently)
I did not inquire.

                    WALDMAN
Suppose you succeed now. Your corpse moved and breathes.
It seems a man. But can Man exist without a soul? Is it
then Man? What is it?

                    VICTOR
Henry - don't - -

                    HENRY
            (To Waldman)
Wrestle with your theological problems as you choose. I am
not interested in souls.

                    WALDMAN
The mere attempt is mortal sin.

                    HENRY

Words! Come, Victor!

                    GOD WILL NOT ALLOW IT!

            (HENRY and VICTOR move screen - carry
            stretcher, covered with sheet, put it
            down R.C. VICTOR steps back. FRITZ
            crouches near machine.

                         HENRY
Dr. Waldman, examine this thing, satisfy yourself and Victor
that it is dead.

                         WALDMAN
I must see this horror through. You will need the priest,
not the master of science, when you come to your senses.
               (Approaches stretcher, draws sheet
               sufficiently on one side to show
               an arm, pause, lifts hand to feel
               pulse, puts head down to listen for
               breathing, steps back)
Of course the thing is dead.

               (Its arm drops limp from sheet as he
               lets go of pulse)

                         HENRY
Look upon its face!
               (They hesitate)

                         VICTOR
No, no.

                         HENRY
Then you, Dr. Waldman!

               (WALDMAN with hesitation and loathing,
               pulls away the cloth from face)

                         WALDMAN
               (Approaches step or two, gazes fascinated)
It is like a death mask.

               (FRITZ attaches discs to head and foot
of stretcher.)

                         VICTOR
What is this for?

                         HENRY
So everything shall be ready - when the lightning strikes!
I have talked of the power of the sun; I can bring those rays
into this machine. But I need another power, immense electrical
power! So what have I done? Attached my machine to the
lightning rod outside the house, tied myself to the storm
clouds, taken the fury of the heavens.

                         VICTOR

You will be Killed!

                        HENRY
Be calm. The lightning runs off harmlessly into the earth.
Fritz knows how to attach the cable and to disconnect it.
            (He is mixing the two bottles he had
            left on the table - he pours one
            colorless liquid into the other, the
            result is a scarlet fluid)
Ready Fritz.

            (FRITZ goes back of the machine
            HENRY brings the bottle of fluid
            pours it down the throat of the
            body)

                        VICTOR
What is that?

                        HENRY
The Elixir, the Elixir of Life. I found some of the formula
in those old black letter books, I worked out the rest myself.
Now we wait - -

            (They approach fascinated)

                        VICTOR
            (Whispers hoarsely)
In the name of religion, Dr. - no! But in the name of
Science - do you want him to succeed?

                        WALDMAN
            (Enthusiastically)
Yes! Yes - no! God forgive me, what am I saying?
            (Silence)
You have failed Henry, and I thank Heaven for it.

            (Pause)
            (Lightning. Machine spits and crackles
            sparks shoots across a gap, all sorts of
            colors and noises)

                        HENRY
            (With a scream)

I have succeeded.
            (The body very slowly clenches and unclenches
            the right hand that has dropped to the side
            of the stretcher, makes a guttural sound,
            half a groan, half a breath, lifts right
            arm stiffly, lifts head a few inches, stares
            at Henry, then drops back. They all stand
            motionless)
            (In wild exaltation)
I have made life, out of matter that was dead!

                        WALDMAN
You make yourself equal with God - that was the sin of the
fallen angel!
                (As CURTAIN falls - he drops
                on knees mumbling over and
                over: "God forgive him.")

                    C U R T A I N

Page Missing 1-22

HENRY
Two years, perhaps a little more. But you cannot follow the
analogy to a human child to closely, for of course he isn't
human --

WALDMAN
Isn't he?

HENRY
(Unheeding)
No a better analogy is to compare him with a puppy, or a
lion's cub. Except that he is beginning to talk. Yesterday,
for instance, but I'll bring him up, and you shall help me
teach him his afternoon lesson.

WALDMAN
Bring him up? Where are you keeping him?

HENRY
(Hesitates)
There's a little cellar under my bedroom --

WALDMAN
You had him upstairs, in the attic.

HENRY
He howled so the other night - I was afraid the neighbors would
be roused and search the place. Besides, Fritz sleeps up
there, and the poor lad is terrified of him.

WALDMAN
But a cellar - a dungeon --
HENRY

(Impatiently)
It's clean and dry enough. Fritz!
(Enter FRITZ from R.F.)
Fritz, go and fetch ---

(Wild motions of protest from FRITZ,
who looks terrified)

WALDMAN
What's the matter with him?

HENRY
Afraid. He pinches him when he can, and once he bit him.
(To Fritz)
Take the whip then, and he'll be meek enough.
(Pours more wine. Exit FRITZ

WALDMAN
I don't like that whip. Must you torture him?

HENRY
(Snaps out)
Is a lion tamer with his whip and hot iron, a torturer? I tell
you he's a lion's cub, he must be afraid of me, he must obey me.

WALDMAN

Have you used the hot iron too?

HENRY
(Evasively)
I will subdue him though intelligence.
> FRITZ bursts in from bedroom in complete terror, ducks for his refuge under the table, somersaulting in his hurry, and dropping the whip on the floor)
> (With nasty laugh)

Fool! I tell you he won't hurt you. If you behave so every time you see him, you'll tempt him to chase you.

WALDMAN

Well, where is your lion cub?

(Pause)

HENRY

Afraid of the light perhaps. I bring him here at night, when no one is about.
> (Pulls curtains over window, room darkens.
> HENRY goes to open bedroom door and calls)

Come here. No one will hurt you.
> (Pause)

Come! Do you hear me?
> (Enter F. the MONSTER, slowly. He is a huge creature, and ghastly to look at. His hair is matted, skin - gray-green, eyes and great mouth, scarlet long gray-green hands. He shuffles instead of walking, with bent shoulder, head swaying meaninglessly from side to side. Dressed in dirty ragged clothes)
> (Unconsciously WALDMAN crosses himself. HENRY, seeing this, laughs)

What! the sign of the cross, Father? Does he look so much worse by day? Or is my Elixir failing, and my beautiful monster rotting before our eyes?
> (Rather hysterical laugh)

Look! We have a new trick to show our professor!
> (Goes toward curtains)

But first, what do you do when you come into my presence, slave!
> (MONSTER, slowly crouches down before Henry)

Right. Sit down!
> (MONSTER does so, on the floor)

Lie down!
> (He does so)

Roll over!
> (He rolls over on the floor)

Stand up!
> (Slowly he raises himself, to a crouching ape-like position.

WALDMAN

He did all this before.

                    HENRY
Hold out your left hand! You right!
          (He goes through all these tricks with
            the contemptuous dignity of a trained
            lion in a circus)
Where is Dr. Waldman?
          (MONSTER slowly turns head towards priest)
Where is your master?
          (His head turns toward Henry)
And Fritz?
          (MONSTER'S back is toward the table, but
            he makes a sudden swift movement, like a
            cat's towards Fritz. A scramble, and
            Fritz scuttles from under table and out
            door R.F.)
Come back here! How dare you. Bring me that whip!

                    WALDMAN
Henry!

                    HENRY
I shan't hurt him.
          (With reluctance, the MONSTER brings whip
            to Henry)
Now look, our new trick! I didn't teach him this.
          (With a quick movement, HENRY throws back
            curtains, admitting the sunlight. MONSTER,
            for a terrified moment scuttles back, then
            eagerly crawls up into the light, and kneels
            there hold up his hands to the sun like
            a savage in prayer, muttering gibberish)

                    WALDMAN
          (Shocked)
He is   praying to the sun!

                    HENRY
Of course. Sun worship -- fire worship -- he is going through
all the instinctive processes of primitive man - both in
religion and behaviour. Growing children do it as well as
savages.

                    WALDMAN
It is the warmth --

                    HENRY
And the feeling of life. Perhaps, Father, he recognizes and
worships the Great Ray, the unseen life-giving Ray which I
caught in my machine.
          *MONSTER turns head, listening)
He is a child of the sun -- and the storm.
          (To Monster)
Fire! Great Fire!

          (At the word "fire" MONSTER shows terror,
            jumps up and cringes)

WALDMAN
Why does he do that?

HENRY
There was once - he was in a rage, he tried to escape. I could not tame him. I had to use a hot iron.

>   (MONSTER is mumbling in terror "fire" and repeatedly touches his side)

WALDMAN
   (Soothingly)
Good fire. Great fire.

>   (MONSTER gets up, goes to window, holds out arms again, draws deep breaths)

HENRY
That is my garden. Say it! Garden!

FRANKENSTEIN
Gar-den.
>   (He points, eager questioning in his motions and his grunts)

HENRY
Trees.

FRANKENSTEIN
Trees!

HENRY
Flowers.

FRANKENSTEIN
Flow-ers!
>   (Looks up, pointing above, with simian gesture)

HENRY
Great soft fire, the sun. Sun.

FRANKENSTEIN
Sun.

HENRY
The blue Heaven, the - sky.

					FRANKENSTEIN
Sky.
					(He continues to gaze, panting
					excited, enraptured)

					HENRY
Come here!
					(FRANKENSTEIN turns, reluctantly)
Kneel! No further off, there!
					(FRANKENSTEIN kneels)
What is this?
					(Puts out hand)

					FRANKENTEIN
Hand.

					HENRY
					(Points to Frankenstein's hand)
And that?

					FRANKENSTEIN
					(Raises hand)
Hand.
					(Looks from his hand to Henry's)
Like .... like ....

					HENRY
What am I?

					FRANKENSTEIN
Man.

					HENRY
Yes, man. What else?

					FRANKENSTEIN
Mas-ter
					(Mumbles to himself)
Mas-ter
					(Gets up, holds out arms again to
					the world without)
Sun - sky - trees.
					(Turns to door, starts for door.
					HENRY bars way, holding whip)

					HENRY
No back!

					WALDMAN
IT is light and air that he wants, like any animal, like any
plant.

					HENRY
					(Imperiously)
Be careful, Dr. Waldman, before this slave here, there must be
only command, blind obedience, no discussion.

					WALDMAN
But surely, Henry, of course you must be stern, but not cruel.

FRANKENSTEIN
(Eagerly questioning)
Cru-el?

HENRY
You have not seen him in his rages, my way is the only way.
You shall go out there in the garden, when it is dark.

FRANKENSTEIN

Dark?

WALDMAN
When the sun goes down. When the great fire goes - no more
fire.

FRANKENSTEIN
(Piteously)
No more ... great fire.

WALDMAN
The great fire will come again. It is begun again ... every
day.

FRANKENSTEIN

Be-gun?

HENRY
Born.

FRANKENSTEIN
Born? Born?
(Thinks, thumps his breast and asks as
question)
Born?

WALDMAN
There is something stirring there.
(To Frankenstein)
There is BEAUTY in the garden, in the world outside, that's
why you want to go there.

FRANKENSTEIN
Beau-ty

WALDMAN

Sun, flowers, trees, the mountains around us - all that is
beauty.

(MONSTER looks outside, drinking in the
sight of this new world)

HENRY
(Triumphant)
Yes, there is something stirring in that queer brain of his.
Perhaps I will be ready in a few weeks. We will take him to
Dr. Kammoern first, think what a subject matter his
lectures!

(MONSTER begins stealthily crouching
like a cat, seeing something through
the window. They turn as FRITZ runs
past the window and opens door, making
excited signs)

WALDMAN

Someone is coming.

HENRY

(To Monster)

Get back in there.

(It is too late, Victor follows Fritz
into house)

WALDMAN

Victor Moritz! When did you come back?

(VICTOR stands horrified and fascinated,
unable to answer. MONSTER, half crouching
watches this new man, partly fear yet
waiting to spring)

HENRY

Welcome back to Goldstadt, Victor! Behold my - monster, whose birth you attended.

VICTOR

My God, Henry.

HENRY

Don't you admire him? Well, perhaps he lacks a little beauty, but he walks, he talks, he even thinks.

VICTOR

(Repeats in awe)

My God!

HENRY

Dr. Waldman wrote you he was alive. Alive, and growing stronger every day - and more intelligent! Look Victor, he does tricks like a puppy!

WALDMAN

Henry, I beg you - not again.

(As FRITZ passes near, MONSTER reaches
round stealthily and nips his leg. A
howl and FRITZ rushes off R.F.)

HENRY

Beast

(Hit's him)

Stand quiet. Now speak, slave, speak. Tell this man you name.

MONSTER
(Sullenly)
Frank-en-stein.

VICTOR
(Gasps)
Frankenstein!

HENRY
Yes, Frankenstein - I made him, I gave him life, he's the emanation of my brain -- isn't it appropriate that I call him Frankenstein?

FRANKENSTEIN
(Timidly)
Master - made -- ?
(Unable to express his idea, he thumps his chest again)
-- made - Franken-stein

HENRY
You see - he thinks. He wishes, early in his intellectual development, to inquire into his own origin -- again like any savage, Dr. Waldman, or like any child. He even has a religion of his own. Victor -- but our priest was shocked at it! Perhaps he was a theory of his birth!
(Turns round to monster)
Frankenstein! Speak! What are you thoughts.

VICTOR
Henry - get rid of him. I must say something to you.

HENRY
In a moment. Frankenstein! What are your thoughts.

FRANKENSTEIN
Thoughts?

HENRY
Yes, talk, speak, use the words I have taught you.

FRANKENSTEIN
(Gestures to Waldman and Victor)
Men ... mas-ters ... like -
(Gestures to Henry)

WALDMAN
Yes, I see what he means, ne's never seen anyone but us, he thought we were the only other men --

FRANKENSTEIN
Other-er?

HENRY
The only men, you mean.

                    FRANKENSTEIN
Man ... other man. But Fran-ken-stein -
          (Gives it up)

                    HENRY
Well, go on.

                    FRANKENSTEIN
Man talk. Fran-en-stein talk.
          (Looks at hands)
Hand like ...
          (Looks at their hands)
hand . Fran-ken-stein not ... man.

                    HENRY
Of course not. You are not a man ...a master ... you must
never think such thoughts or I shall punish you.

          (FRANKENSTEIN cringes)

                    WALDMAN
Not a man, but you are like a man.

                    FRANKENSTEIN
          (Eagerly)
Like? Like?

                    HENRY
          (Drawing Waldman aside)
Doctor, you must not say such things. There is no mirror in
this house, I have destroyed them all. He doesn't know what
he's like - if he did! Don't you see it might be hard to
control him?

                    WALDMAN
You cannot keep this up, Henry. You are dealing, not with
your lion-cub, your trained dog, or whatever you have called
him, but a creature with a mind. You are growing hysterical.
You are beginning to hate him - it is he who has the right to
hate - - -

                    FRANKENSTEIN
          (Overhearing)
Hate? Hate?
          (They turn and are silent)

Hate ... hurt ...
          (Glaring at Henry)
hurt Frankenstein.

                    VICTOR
For heaven's sake, Henry, get him away. I must talk to you.

                    WALDMAN
          (Gently)
Frankenstein, come here.
          (Goes with him to window, pointing out objects
           outside. FRANKENSTEIN at once eager and docile)

VICTOR
Your father drove back with me.

HENRY
Good God! Where is he?

VICTOR
At the Inn in the Square. I couldn't help it, henry.

HENRY
He'll come up here any minute.

VICTOR
No, but he might come soon. He has to see the horses are put up first, and that Amelia is comfortably settled.

HENRY
Amelia, did she come too?

VICTOR
Yes, Katrina asked her to. In heaven's name, why didn't you write them? I begged you to.

HENRY
What could I write? These past three weeks - -

VICTOR
You could write the truth to me. If I'd known - - anything at all, I might have kept them from worrying. All I know was in a note from Dr. Waldman - that the creature was alive. They've come to take you home.

HENRY
Fritz!
(FRITZ comes from the door R.F.)
Go through to the front of the house - watch for a carriage, for a man, a big man - -

VICTOR
Or a man with a girl.

HENRY
If you see anyone, come quickly through the garden and tell me.
(Exit FRITZ, R.F. FRANKENSTEIN makes
a quick movement at him, he scuttles off -
WALDMAN calls, "Frankenstein" and he
turns meekly again to the window)
What shall I do? I'm trapped now, trapped. My father would not understand, Amelia would be terrified. Or would she - - - - ? After all, I did this to make myself great, and to make her proud of me. She'd understand. And I'm almost ready to let the whole world see my monster.

VICTOR
Not the way he looks now - nor the way you look. Get him away somewhere, then wash and change your clothes. Where do you keep him?

HENRY

In the cellar.

VICTOR

The darker the better! Get him in there and make yourself look decent. Your father will be angry enough that I ran away the minute we reached the Inn.

HENRY

What a fool I've been! I never thought they'd come here. Frankenstein!
   (MONSTER turns)
Get back in there!
   (FRANKENSTEIN hesitates, points pathetically
   outside)
Back in there! Do you hear!
   (Raises whip)
   FRANKENSTEIN watches whip, measures
   distance to door with his eye, then
   makes a leap for freedom. HENRY jumps
   at him, others rush to help. HENRY has
   hands on Frankenstein's throat. Before
   they can reach the struggle, FRANKENSTEIN
   grasps his wrists and throws Henry off,
   and almost to the floor. HENRY staggers
   to his feet.
His hands are like steel, he could kill us all.

FRANKENSTEIN
   (Fiercely, questioning, but questioning
   triumphantly)
Kill? KILL? KILL!!

HENRY
   (Recovering himself, picks up whip
   strikes Frankenstein violently with
   butt)
Slave; dog! How dare you throw me down.

   (FRANKENSTEIN steps back, shrinks a little
   but does not cringe as before)

FRANKENSTEIN

Throw down!
   (Touches himself, points to master and
   then to floor)
Mas-ter! Down!
   (He pulls himself up as others watch
   him fascinated and alarmed)
Hand! Like man and ... arm -
   (Feels his arms and body, looking at them,
   feels his chest, measures the others with
   his eyes as he slowly realizes his own
   size and strength.

HENRY
   (Raising whip)
Down - down on the ground!

(FRANKENSTEIN, looks at him with hate,
meditating defiance, then crouches
slowly, unwillingly, like lion before
trainer)

VICTOR

There's Fritz - -
(FRITZ appears in garden)

HENRY

(Hastily)
Go in there, Frankenstein.

(FRANKENSTEIN rises sullenly turns
to window)

FRANKENSTEIN

Fire, great fire - sun.
(Henry raises whip again. FRANKENSTEIN
sullenly shambles off)

VICTOR

Go in yourself - stay there - until you make yourself look decent.

(Exit HENRY as BARON appears
in garden)
I must get rid of him.

WALDMAN

We'll take Henry to him.
(BARON stands in the door, a large man
of the country squire type, unusually
good natured, rather red faced and
angry now)

VICTOR

Ah - come in, Baron. You found your way here quickly.

BARON

No, thanks to you, who turned and ran off while I was back in the stable. You develop queer manners when you return to your university.

VICTOR

I'm sorry, Baron. I thought I'd find Henry and bring him to the Inn to save you coming up the hill.

FRITZ looks in timidly, seen room
clear, enters and finishes clearing
table)

BARON

You might have said so.

VICTOR

Permit me to introduce Dr. Waldman, our head professor of Anatomy.

BARON
(Genial at once)

I am honored, Dr. Waldman. Henry has spoken a lot in praise of you.

WALDMAN

Thank you.

BARON

Well, I'm glad to see that, though you may be a professor of anatomy, you are not likely to teach our boys this new atheistical nonsense. I hope you see to it that they don't read books by those scoundrels, Rousseau and Voltaire. They started that Revolution in France.

WALDMAN
(Gently, smiling)

You are not in favor of the higher education, Baron?

I never was. It was his mother's idea, letting the boy stuff his head full of books from the time he was a baby. But where is he?

VICTOR

He's not here, Baron.

BARON

That's obvious.
(Looks around)
A queer looking place for the lad to live in. What's through there?
(Points to barred door)
It is barred like a strong room.
(Knocks)

VICTOR

That's his bedroom, and beyond that his - workshop.

(BARON tries door)

BARON

It's locked.
(Knocks louder)
Then maybe he's in his work-shop, as you call it, and doesn't hear.

(There is a faint rattling of chains
which the DOCTOR hears for he moves
nervously)

WALDMAN
The windows are shut, I saw them as I came up the hill. I'll
find him and bring him to the Inn, Baron, if you'll wait there.

BARON
What, walk down that hill in this heat, when I've just walked
up? Thanks, I'll wait here.
(Sits disgusted - kicks at some books
on floor)

VICTOR
He's probably at a lecture.

WALDMAN
(Quickly)
There's Dr. Kammeren's lecture this afternoon. Henry never
likes to miss them.

VICTOR OF COURSE, THAT'S WHERE HE'D BE.

BARON
Lecture? Where is it? Does it mean I have to wait for hours?

VICTOR
He lectures in the anatomical class room. It's the white
building, just beyond the Inn, on a small side street that runs
past the stables.

BARON
A rifle shot from where we stopped. I'll go find him there.
(Stops on way to door and looks
suspiciously at them)
There's something queer - - why did you rush up here at once,
without saying a word to either of us, Victor?
(VICTOR has no ready reply)
Dr. Waldman, are you waiting for my son?

WALDMAN
Uh - no. I wanted to talk to victor.

BARON
(Laughs jovially)
Oh, you're in for a wigging, are you, my boy? Not so easy to
deal with those lazy lads, is it Doctor, when they got too
old to have the cane applied to their tails? Well, I shall
see you later at the inn, Victor. Meantime - -
(To Fritz)
get his things packed.

WALDMAN
(Agitated, as BARON is going out)
You're not asking him to go home with you, are you Baron?

BARON
         (Surprised)
Ask him? No, I'm not asking him, I'm taking him home.
         (Looking from one to the other)
What is there so surprising in this? Is the lad never to have a holiday? From all you tell me, he needs one badly

         (As BARON disappears, grumbling,
         "asking him indeed" VICTOR and
         WALDMAN look at each other in
         consternation.

WALDMAN
My God forgive me for the lies I have told that man!

         (Tension relaxes)

VICTOR
We're safe for an hour. And Henry had better be got home.

WALDMAN
In a few weeks he'll be ready.

VICTOR
In a few days he'll have his mother and sister Katrina over here, as well.

WALDMAN
But what about Frank - -

VICTOR
My God, he's not going to let a creature like that live - is he?
         (Knocks on door)
Henry, your father has gone, come out.
         (Door is unlocked from other side, enter
         HENRY looking as before)
Good God, man, you can't be taken down to the Inn looking like this. Don't you understand - your father is here and Amelia. They've come to take you home!

HENRY
How can I go home! I'm only partly finished - I made a living body, now I am developing a mind - - I must not be interrupted.

VICTOR
But Amelia - - -

HENRY
I told you before, she must wait. Everything must wait - until I am satisfied with my experiment.

VICTOR
No woman will wait forever for a man who neither writes her nor bothers to see her.

HENRY

Oh, I understand! You've been in Belrive, you've been with her every day. Have you persuaded her to break with me, to go back to you?

WALDMAN

Henry, mu son! You know Victor better - -

HENRY

Perhaps she's come here to tell me she wants you!

VICTOR
(Savagely)

Perhaps she has then!

HENRY

You - - you call yourself my friend, you asked for friendship again, that - that last last night here. Amelia has been living in my house, in the care of my father and mother. You rode over there daily, you - - -

VICTOR
(To Waldman)

Father! I never once saw her alone. I never spoke a word of love - -

HENRY

It does not matter! - - I won her away from you once, I can win her again.

WALDMAN

My sons, you must not quarrel.

VICTOR
(Angry)

What can he offer her now? To live in a house - with that thing in the cellar - - to stay under the roof with a creature who looks like - -

HENRY

By that time, I'll be done with my - experiment. I let the beating heart stop, when I had learned all I could from it. I reburied the man in the mountains. When I have learned all I want to from Frankenstein
(Gesture of killing)

VICTOR

Thank heaven! But do it now!

WALDMAN

No!

HENRY
(Continues to Dr. Waldman)

God created life. I created life! God gives life and God gives death too.

WALDMAN
To blasphemy, would you add murder?

HENRY
(Speaks reasonably, quietly)
Murder, Dr. Waldman? What is murder? You said, the Church says, that man is created in the image of God, but the Church doesn't mean that God has arms and legs. God gives man part of himself when He breathes into him a soul. Isn't that good theology. Well then, I've mocked God by giving life when I cannot give a soul.

WALDMAN
(Sternly)
Thou shalt not kill.

HENRY
thou shalt not kill men - men wit souls. The commandments say nothing about killing beasts, or monsters without souls. What has my monster got to do with God?

VICTOR
Damned little, to my thinking.

HENRY
You see, you can't have it both ways, Father! If this thing that I made has no soul, it not human, it's a beast, and a beast can be killed without sin!

WALDMAN
Who am I to know what relation God has decreed between you and this thing that you and the Devil, your rays and your Elixir brought into the world. But it is linked to you more strongly than son to father. And this I know, that it is part of yourself and that you cannot destroy the unholy life that you have dared to breathe into that body.

HENRY
Then it will destroy me.

WALDMAN
(turns away. HENRY'S remark strikes him
deeply and he seems to agree, as he turns
back to Henry)
This is in God's hands.

(Sounds of chains and a sudden howl from below)

(THE EGOTIST AGAIN)
But do you think that I will let it? No, in a few weeks, a living, thinking man, created by man, he goes to Dr. Kammeren and becomes the scientific wonder of all ages -- and I the greatest figure in the history of -

(They have their backs to the door, and
do not see the BARON until he speaks
from the doorway)

BARON

Henry!

HENRY

Father -

BARON
(After long look, turns on Waldman)
So this is what you make of your students, Dr. Waldman! A fine healthy lad I sent you, and now, the boy looks like a maniac.

VICTOR

I said he'd - he'd been overworking, Baron.

BARON
(Turning on Victor)
I went to that lecture place where you told me Henry had gone, and an old professor with whiskers said -
(Imitation German accent)
he hadn't been near his classes in weeks and spends all his time up here.
(to Henry)
Where were you just now, sir?

HENRY

I was reading, father.

BARON

But that the door was locked, and Dr. Waldman here said you weren't here.
(To Waldman)
If you'd let me give that door a few healthy kicks I'd have saved myself a walk down that confounded hill.;
(TO Henry)
Why do you have your rooms barred with that great thing as though it were a strong-box?

HENRY

To prevent myself being disturbed... uh! Students.

BARON

What in the devil is this great whip doing here?
(Picks up whip)

(WALDMAN and VICTOR alarmed)

HENRY

It belongs to a carter, who has been doing some odd jobs about the house. He forgot it when he left.
(BARON drops whip)

Dr. Waldman, are you sure you didn't know the poor lad was here all the time? Were you trying to keep his father from seeing him?

HENRY
I was asleep, father, I was enjoying a most refreshing sleep.

BARON
You look it.
   (To Waldman)
It seems to me, sir, that when a father comes all this distance to visit his son, he's not to be fobbed off and lied to because the lad's asleep.

WALDMAN
I was at fault, Baron. I owe you an apology.

BARON
   (To Henry)
Bur you said just now you were reading.

HENRY
Yes, I had been asleep, then I picked up a book.

BARON
My reception here seems a little strange.

HENRY
Father, there was no discourtesy intended. Tell me the news from home. How are mother and Katrina?

BARON
I thought there was something queer about this. You'll see tonight! I got fresh post horses at the Inn; Amelia is in the carriage. We're going at once.

HENRY
Father - I want to - I'd like to -- but I can't - not just now.

BARON
You can't! Where's that dumb servant of his? Fritz!
   (FRITZ appears with an old fashioned leather bag)
There - you're packed. I'll give you three minutes to change you clothes and come.

   (AMELIA stands in the open door)

May I come in?

   (Silence - AMELIA shocked at his
   appearance)
Henry! Henry!
   (She runs towards him)

HENRY
Father, don't judge me, and don't misjudge my friends. You cannot understand, just yet. But please, since Amelia is here, leave me alone with her -- all of you.

BARON
All the explaining you want to do, can be done in the carriage on our way back ---

                        HENRY
No, I must talk to her now - and here. Please father - -

                        WALDMAN
            (Taking Baron's arm)
Baron, I understand you very justified indignation, but the
truth is experiments in natural science have overwrought you
son. We have all done our best to get him to take a rest, I
myself a few weeks ago was urging him to go home, etc......

            (He walks Baron out L.)

            (VICTOR looks from Amelia to Henry
            and to door R. anxiously)

                        AMELIA
Go after them, Victor, help to calm the Baron.
            (As VICTOR hesitates)
Do go!

            (Exit VICTOR R. after last look at
            door R.)

            (Pause. They look at each other)

            (At length)

Henry!

                        HENRY
Nothing's the matter with me, Amelia. I've been working too
hard, that's all.
            (He goes to kiss her, she draws back)
            (He kisses her hand)
I'm sorry, I forgot - I must look terrible.

                        AMELIA
You look ill. Don't you know that?

                        HENRY
Do I? I haven't - there are no mirrors - so I could not see - -
am I so - - repellant?
            (Looks at his hands, his clothes)
Or had you some other reason for drawing away from me - just
now.

                        AMELIA
            (Hesitates)
No - no reason. I did not mean to draw away.
            (Kisses him reluctantly)

                        HENRY
Victor's been home with you - at Belrive. He's quite the dandy,
with his Viennese clothes and Paris finery. He's - -

                        AMELIA
            (Interrupts with a giggle)
He's a little cleaner than you, Henry.
            (They both laugh)

HENRY
My hands and clothes are stained with chemicals. Laboratory work is dirtier than a kitchen maid's, and often not as useful.
          (Holds out his hand. With a little
          reluctance she gives hers)
Amelia, it is like being in heaven to see you.
          (She laughs a little)

AMELIA
Heaven was not so far away --

HENRY
I could not come.

AMELIA
Victor wrote me frequently. Such interesting letters about his travels.

HENRY
Victor again! Amelia, I have been doing such terrific work, such amazing work ---

AMELIA
That it left you no time, not even a minute - for me? To write "I love you" on a sheet of paper does not take very long.

HENRY
          (He does this sort of thing very
          easily and well)
Had I begun to write that I would never have stopped. I would have gone on and on, writing Amelia I love, Amelia, I love you, I adore --

AMELIA
And there would have been no terrific work accomplished?

HENRY
          (Suddenly serious)
You know my work comes first - always, always. I told you that, when we became engaged. You said you loved me more for feeling that way. But during the first weeks -- after I returned -- after Victor had quarreled with me and had gone away -- you wanted a letter everyday, a visit every week --

AMELIA
I did not get them.

HENRY
No, I know that. For almost as soon as I returned here, I began -- I began some studies and experiments which - which had to take up every minute of my time. Everything else had to be excluded, friends, love - there was not enough time for work.

AMELIA
How could I know that? Your mother and father grew more an more worried -- I had plenty of faith at first. But even faith can starve.

HENRY

I was working for you. Your face was always near me, when
I sat with my books, or when I lay down at night. I felt
your cool hands when I was tired -- Amelia, you don't believe
me. But I will show you. I have done something - so extra-
ordinary - something no man has ever done before. I shall be
the greatest scientific figure in the world. and you shall
share my glory. We'll go - all over the world. You shall be
feted, flattered -- I want a few more weeks to myself. Then --

AMELIA

What have you done?

HENRY

You'll see - you'll understand.
> (Goes toward door, R.F. calls)

Fritz! Go into my bedroom and unlock that other door.
> (Offstage noise of a bar and lock being
> undone. FRITZ enters quickly, goes to
> fireplace.

You have heard me talk of creating life -- wait. Look!

> (FRANKENSTEIN shambles in, hunched but
> not as much as before. AMELIA screams.
> He stands there looking dumbly at her)

AMELIA

Henry! What is it? What have you done?

HENRY

I have created life.

AMELIA

It is a corpse. It is dead.

HENRY

Nonsense, it is alive. Frankenstein --

AMELIA

Frankenstein!

HENRY

I gave it my name.

AMELIA

Frankenstein! It looks like you.

FRANKENSTEIN

Like ... Master?

HENRY
> (With sardonic fetish)

Have I created a man in my own image! Stand still there,
Frankenstein, while I look at you. At least I did not flatter
myself.

AMELIA

Henry, take him away. I'm frightened.

FRANKENSTEIN

Fri-ghtened?

HENRY

Frightened? He's harmless. He's - like a tiger-cub. I only need the whip - in case he wants to escape, or to snap at Fritz. He'll play tricks for you, talk for you -- I only want a few more weeks to train him. Then Dr. Kammeren gets him, and then I can leave Goldstadt, and you Belrive, and we'll go away -
   (He sees that she is badly frightened)
I'm sorry, Amelia. He is gruesome -- I wasn't thinking of his beauty when I worked over him.

AMELIA

You boasted - in Belrive - you could create -- you've not done it!

HENRY

I have --

AMELIA

It is terrible!

HENRY

You loved me because I said I could do it - now I have. Now you must love me -

FRANKENSTEIN

You -- not man?
   (Vague gestures, moaning what are you.
   He takes a step towards her)

AMELIA

Don't come near me! You- Henry, take him away!

HENRY

Go back there, Frankenstein.
   (FRANKENSTEIN turns sullen, stands still)
Back!
   (He does not move. HENRY seizes whip from
   floor)

AMELIA
   (Now in compete terror)
If you've created - destroy it. It's loathsome, it's horrible.

HENRY

But it's wonderful. Amelia, you always loved me when I talked of doing wonderful things. Look, I have done something wonderful - more wonderful than anything man has attempted so far.

AMELIA

No! It's -- I can't bear it --
   (In her fright, she runs and clings to him.
   He puts his arms around her and kisses her.
   This arouses FRANKENSTEIN who with a sudden
leap, reaches them and pulls them apart.

FRANKENSTEIN

No! Frankenstein want - - -

HENRY

Back, back, you vile creature. You dare to touch a woman - -

FRANKENSTEIN
(Triumphantly)

Wo-man! WO-MAN! ... beauty ... woman ...

HENRY
(To Amelia)

Get out of here.
    (Hits FRANKENSTEIN, with butt of whip on
    head. FRANKENSTEIN unheeds this, but
    continues to gaze hungrily at Amelia)
    (Screaming)

Down, down at my feet.
    FRANKENSTEIN contemptuously flings him
    off)

Amelia - go - go - for God's sake.
    She is half fainting with fear. FRITZ
    comes from fireplace, seizes her hand -
    starts pulling her to door. With a
    scream, she comes to - both go off
    running)

FRANKENSTEIN

Wo-man ... Frankenstein want - -

HENRY

Slave .. at your master's feet.
    (FRANKENSTEIN looks at him unmoved)
    (HENRY, afraid, starts toward door.
    FRANKENSTEIN with a sudden leap, catches
    and drags him back)

FRANKENSTEIN

Master! Where is the woman?
    (Shakes him. HENRY gasps almost
    inaudibly, "down at your master's -
    FRANKENSTEIN ironically, fiendishly)
Master! Master! I am YOUR master now.

    (Shaking him as Curtain falls)

C U R T A I N

ACT II

SCENE: Main hall of the Baron's house at Belrive. Large open folding windows rear lead to a balcony, with treetops and a distant view of the lake and mountains. Doorway R. to entrance stairs, door left, closed, to rest of house. A large table with bowl of roses, couch R., cage with three doves at window rear. Parcels, boxes, etc. on side table.

The time is four months later.

AT RISE: AMELIA and VICTOR are standing at window rear, looking over the lake. They have been quarreling.

VICTOR
(Coming down stage)
Very well, then there is no more to be said.

AMELIA
Victor, dear Victor...
(She follows him down)
..please don't feel badly.

VICTOR

What can you expect?

AMELIA
Don't be cross with me -- not today, of all days.

VICTOR
Do you want me to go away - now? I will, if it will please you.

AMELIA
No, no. Please! Henry would feel terrible. He wouldn't understand.

VICTOR
(Half sits on table)
Of course he'd understand. HE knows as well as you that I've always loved you and always will. He know I went all over Europe because I couldn't bear to see him, and couldn't bear to think of you.

AMELIA
(Sits on couch)
I know. And when you did come back, I was ----

                    VICTOR

You had changed again. You were the old Amelia who loved
me, and not the Henry who never wrote you, who never came
back here to Belrive to see you. Then at Goldstadt - - -

                    AMELIA

I went with you and the Baron that time not because Katrina
begged me, but because I meant to tell him - -

                    VICTOR

To tell him what!

                    AMELIA

That I wasn't sure, after all, that I loved him.

                    VICTOR

But you didn't tell him

                    AMELIA
            (Troubled)
No...No. He looked so tired and ill, I was so sorry. I didn't
know how to begin. Then- - -he brought out that horrible creat-
ture- - -and after that I don't know what I said. He kept repeating that he'd made good his boast to me- - -

                    VICTOR

What boast?

                    AMELIA

He'd boasted, when he was here, that he'd create - a living
man. He said I had loved him for that, and therefore I must
love him because he had done it. And all the time that thing
stood there. I wanted to tell him I hated him for what he'd
done. But I don't remember anything until I came out of my
faint and saw your face bending above me.
            (Pause)
Don't you see now, Victor?

                    VICTOR

Of course, I see that. And that you couldn't break with him
during the weeks that followed, when we were afraid of brain
fever.

                    AMELIA

Then why are you quarreling with me now?

                    VICTOR

You twist my words around. I'm not quarreling with you, Amelia
dear.

                    AMELIA

Aren't you?

                    VICTOR

You know I'm not. I want you to be happy. I'll go away, all
over Europe again, if you want, or I'll stay here and help you
nurse Henry back to health, if he needs it. Haven't I don
both those things already?

AMELIA
I never doubted you love, or your generosity.

VICTOR
I've been arguing with you because you have changed so often, I don't think you know your own mind. You were sweet to him when he was sick, and needed all your love to get well- - -

AMELIA
How romantic you are, Victor! I'm afraid he needed nothing of the sort. The day Fritz came and told him he'd seen that monster fall over a cliff in the mountains, he recovered at once.

VICTOR
The relief he felt then helped, of course. But it was obvious to everyone during those weeks, that no matter how tender and sweet you were to him, you were not in love with him, and were not going to marry him.

AMELIA
Obvious to everyone but him.

VICTOR
And then, when I went back to Goldstadt, you practically told me that you would write me n a week, saying the engagement was broken. Do you blame me for living there, hoping- - -

AMELIA
I know...I'm sorry.

VICTOR
When I got the letter finally it was to tell me that you were gong to marry him- - -today.

AMELIA
I know, I must seem like some hateful, cruel coquette, like some of those cold-hearted grand ladies you met in the great cities while you were away. I'm not like that. You see - I do love you, Victor. I always have, too. When we became betrothed, that day at my father's bedside. I was thrilled though I was only twelve, and I was happy though I knew my father was dying.

VICTOR
In six years you have outgrown the feeling. Six years can be a long time.

AMELIA
No- - -only when Henry came back here a year ago with his big flashing eyes, his lovely nervous hands, his wonderful talk-- he made all life exciting. With us, you know that life is a pleasant but dull routine. We work and ride, and talk about our herds and farms, and read silly love stories and go to bed because we're bored. Then Henry comes; he talks of the wonderful future, yet he's even then making those wonders real. When he talks of the work he has done and is going to do, fairy tales are commonplace stories, and magic is an everyday occurance.

VICTOR
And he's the great magician. I know, he makes me feel very
small and insignificant.

AMELIA
And myself too. I want only to adore him and wait on him and
be of use to him---when he is in that mood.

VICTOR
Then the mood must have come back, after I left.

AMELIA
It did, that's just what happened. When he looks at me, and
is so sure he can make me love him, I am helpless, I do love
him.

VICTOR
Well, then, there is no more to be said. I'll be in Goldstadt, and afterwards, I shall go to Vienna to live, or Paris.
Perhaps I shall see you there, when you come with Henry, you'll
be a great lady.

AMELIA
No, for he's to give up his science. We'll be living here,
just dull country folks. I had hoped --

VICTOR
What?

AMELIA
That Katrina - that you and Katrina --

VICTOR
Katrina? She's a child. She's fourteen.

AMELIA
In two years, three years -- you'll have forgotten you loved
me - and she'll be grown up. She loves you --

VICTOR
It's absurd. She's a child. She always will seem like a child
- or an angel. It's impossible to think of things like marriage, with Katrina

AMELIA
Why? She's practical enough, for all her unworldliness. She's
taken charge of all the wedding arrangements -- Besides, she
adores Henry, and --

                    VICTOR
None of it's any reason for marrying her to Henry's best friend.
No, I can't settle down on the estate next to yours, and ride
placidly past your home each day - not even with an angel for
a wife.

                    AMELIA
Katrina loves you.

                    VICTOR
For heaven's sake, don't keep repeating that, Amelia. Or I
will think you are like one of those heartless coquettes you
spoke of. Katrina knows nothing of love. If she did love me,
as you imply, it's all the more reason why I should never come
here again.

                    AMELIA
            (With a slight catch in her voice)
Never?

                    VICTOR
            (Suddenly determined)
I ride back to Goldstadt tonight, from the church. This is
goodbye - - for a long time.
            (He crosses to her, kidded her gently
             and goes back to his place by the table)
Take care of Henry, and keep him from any more long
spells of work or his health and nerves will be ruined.
            (At the end of this, enter the BARON, in
             hunting coat, with gun and game bag. Slings
             off bag and puts gun in corner as he talks)

                    BARON
Well said, Victor Moritz. That nest of lunatics and priests
would poison anybody's mind. I take some small credit to
myself for going back there with you and getting him out of
their clutches. Raving about monsters he'd made up out of
ash cans! '

                    VICTOR
            (laughs)
Goldstadt never did me any harm, Baron.

                    BARON
You! Their devilment rolled off YOU like water off a duck's
back. I know the reason. You don't read their books, and you
never listen to their infernal lectures.
            (Goes up to Amelia, kisses her, arm around her)
This is what my boy needs, and now he's going to get it. How
is our little bride today?

                    AMELIA
Very well, Baron, thank you. Did you have any luck this morning?

BARON
Couldn't hit a thing. They ran away and laughed at me.
(Enter KATRINA R, slender, blonde, fragile
girl of 14 or 15; very grave and candid and
childlike. She is followed by FRITZ, carrying boxes and baskets)
KATRINA
Hello, father. We called to you from the road, but you didn't
hear us. Fritz, take those up to my sitting room, please, and
give them to the woman there.

(Exit FRITZ, L.)

BARON
(To Fritz as he goes)
Then come back, I shall want you.
(To Katrina)
Where have you left the bridegroom - at the church?

KATRINA
No, he came back with us. He stopped at the stables to see
that the horses were ready. He is to ride down first, with
Victor, then you and Amelia and myself in the coach, and Fritz
is to follow in the old carriage, with Helene and the two sew-
ing women. The other servants have gone.

BARON
And where's your mother?

AMELIA
She stayed at the church, she'll wait there for us. Oh,
Amelia, you can't think how lovely it looks. They're filling
it with flowers, masses of them, and mother is showing them
how to arrange everything. They are making a bower for you and
Henry to stand under, and garlands around the pillars. I never
saw anything so beautiful.

AMELIA
(Touched)
You are being so good to me, even your village women. And I
am taking Henry away from you.

KATRINA
Not so very far away. And we'll be busy looking after each
other, father and mother and I.

(Enter HENRY, R., no longer the wild
dishevelled youth of Act I, properly
dressed and comparatively calm)

BARON
Cheer up, my boy, getting married isn't like being hanged.

HENRY
(Laughs)
I'm cheerful, father.

AMELIA
(Laughing)
A gallant speech, Baron.

BARON
(To Amelia)
Men are all like this. There's something inside us that makes us dread the altar. Have you ever seen how an ox pulls back on the rope when you try and drag him into the slaughter house?

KATRINA
(Slightly shocked)
You know father's little ways, Victor.

HENRY crosses to Amelia, puts arm around her. VICTOR turns his back to them. picks up gun, looks at it. FRITZ comes in again, L.)

HENRY
Any luck this morning, father?

(KATRINA crosses stage, pulls bell-rope)

BARON
Couldn't hit a thing. The luck's with you today, my boy.
(VICTOR puts gun back in corner)
Ah---our love birds! Well, I must change my coat for the wedding, and so must you, Victor. Fritz, come and pull off my boots for me. Are you coming, Victor?
(The three exit L. as HELENE enters R)

KATRINA
Helene, go to the Baroness' room, and begin packing her dress. It's on your bed. Heinrich is waiting for it in the courtyard, he's to take it to her.

HELENE
Very good. Am I to go with him and help her ladyship dress?

KATRINA
No, you must stay here and help us. Be quick now.)

(HELENE exits L. HENRY remains standing, arm around Amelia R. KATRINA L. KATRINA looks at them)

I wonder if I've forgotten anything?
(Begins gathering up parcels on the side table)

AMELIA
You are doing too much, Katrina. You'll tire yourself.

KATRINA
No, everything is ready now. They'll be waiting for me with
your dress though. There were two more tiny things -- I told
them to wait until I came. I five or ten minutes you must
come and try it on.

AMELIA
But we need not dress just yet.

KATRINA
I know. But I must be sure it is perfect. Everything must
be perfect for Amelia.
     (Exit L.)

HENRY
Then come back and let me see you!

AMELIA
Oh no, I think it out to be a surprise for you. You won't
know your country Amelia at the altar, dressed u like a great
lady from Versailles or Vienna. The trouble Katrina has taken-
the stuffs from Paris - the consultations -

HENRY
Then you MUST come back. Too many people will be in the
church, I shan't be able to admire you. I'll be too nervous
anyway. Besides, I want to tell Katrina how beautifully she
has done it.

AMELIA
Henry, she's worked so hard, with those two old seamstresses -
as though it were to be her own wedding dress. She wouldn't
even let me help. She - Henry, I've been talking to Victor.

HENRY
     (Quickly)
What about?

AMELIA
Katrina. He does love her, but i wish he loved her differently.
He thinks of her as something scarcely human.

HENRY
I know, Amelia
     (Going to cage)
Nothing would make me so happy, but it will never be. She's
not a woman to him. I think she never will be to any man.
She's -- like one of her own doves.

AMELIA
But that's wrong. Life can't be like that. She loves him.

                    HENRY
She's so young. Victor idealizes her. but --

                    AMELIA
But --? I'm glad I'm not your ideal.

                    HENRY
My wife, today, this afternoon, in a few hours.
          (Kisses her)

                    AMELIA
Happy?

                    HENRY
Yes!

                    AMELIA
Not afraid?

                    HENRY
Not of anything.

                    AMELIA
Neither am I

          (Kiss)

And there are to be no more of those terrible studies?

                    HENRY
          (Agitated)
No, never. Don't talk about them, Amelia. I can't bear it.

                    AMELIA
Of course I won't. But you're sure you'll be contented. just
with me?

                    HENRY
Only with you, only with you. There can be no other happiness,
no other life...I couldn't live without you. That's a thing
lovers say, but it was never so true before.

                    AMELIA
Somehow I can't think of you as a country squire, settling
down on the place the Baron has given us, with a squire's
small interests, hunting and cattle and tenants.

                    HENRY
It will be peace, it will be heaven. We shall have each
other. And there will be books; poetry, romance, history.
But no science, no SCIENCE! And in the years to come, we shall
have our children.

AMELIA

Yes.

HENRY

You're sure you're not still worried, about...that time?

AMELIA

No.

HENRY

You came back and saved me, but for you I should have gone out of my mind.

AMELIA

Even though it happened four months ago. I still wake up at night and see that man. Sometimes he is looking at me, in your rooms, and sometimes groping past me as I stood behind the wall, before Victor found me.

HENRY

Don't, don't , please.

AMELIA

It doesn't matter now. Fritz saw him fall. Henry, let's go down to the lake, where you first told me you loved me. There will be so much excitement as soon as we leave here - you won't seem to belong to me at all.

HENRY

Until we are alone again tonight.

(Enter KATRINA and HELENE with a large box.

AMELIA

Oh, the dress - - I can't go.

(To Katrina...smiles at her)
You may, for a few minutes. Then come up to my room.

(They go out balcony and off L)

KATRINA

You must tell Heinrich to hurry.
        (There is a knock off stage R.)
Go see who that is.

(HELENE off R. KATRINA busy tying up
box. HELENE enters R. again with DR.
WALDMAN. He looks tired and wears
dusty riding cloak. He is talking

2-11

WALDMAN
But it is Henry Frankenstein I wish to see, pray do not disturb - - -

KATRINA
I am Henry's sister. Can I do anything?
    (Gives box to HELENE who exits R.)

WALDMAN
You are the little Katrina?

KATRINA
And you are Dr. Waldman, aren't you? - - You want to see Henry?

WALDMAN
Please. Where is he?

KATRINA
He has just gone down to the lake.

WALDMAN
Alone - is he alone?

KATRINA
Amelia is with him.

WALDMAN
Is the wedding over?

AMELIA
No, it is this afternoon. You are just tin time.

WALDMAN
Thank Heaven.

    VICTOR comes in, wearing new, dressy coat)

VICTOR
Dr. Waldman.

WALDMAN
Victor Moritz!

VICTOR
You look exhausted. Katrina, send Helene with some wine.

KATRINA
I'll bring it.
    (Exits R.)

VICTOR
Let me take you cloak. Have you ridden today from Goldstdt?

                          WALDMAN
Goldstadt, without a halt.

                          VICTOR
You wrote Henry you couldn't come. What has --

                          WALDMAN
They must not be married, my son.

                          VICTOR
Why not? Do you mean --

                          WALDMAN
They must NOT be married.

                          VICTOR
But it's too late, everything is arranged. Father, even if
what Henry did was a mortal sin, as you think, there must be
forgiveness. They love each other.

          (Enter KATRINA with tray, bottle of wine
          and glasses - which she puts on table)

                          KATRINA
Now I'll go find Henry for you, Dr. Waldman.
          (Exits on balcony. VICTOR pours glass
          of wine for DOCTOR which he sips, sitting
          exhausted in chair)

                          WALDMAN
How much have you told Henry of what has been going on these
past four months?

                          VICTOR
Nothing, father. You wrote me about these attacks and
murders, but I said nothing. It would have driven him out
of his head. It was hard enough anyway, trying to make him
well again.

                          WALDMAN
How much does the Baron know?

                          VICTOR
Nothing. None of the family knows anything. They thought
he was raving with fever. When Fritz came with his news, he
saw Henry alone. And the family simply thought he'd got over
his fever.

                          WALDMAN
Then you returned to Goldstadt, and I told you in detail all
I have learned.

                          VICTOR
But there was no conclusive evidence.

WALDMAN
There is evidence enough now!

VICTOR
But Fritz saw --

WALDMAN
Sic weeks ago, he saw him leap or fall over a high cliff, far up the Weissenberg. I too believed the monster dead - because I wanted to believe it. But he is NOT dead.
   (VICTOR jumps up, horrified)

VICTOR
Oh, God! And we thought he'd soon forget.

WALDMAN
Amelia's parents are dead. You love her too, therefore the responsibility for her fate is partly yours. Forget while this monster lives.

VICTOR
God cannot be the Old Testament tyrant you thin Him. God is Love, God is Mercy. He must have pity.

WALDMAN
He is also just. Sin must be punished.

VICTOR
You loved Henry, once.

WALDMAN
I love him now. But a curse is on him, he must not bring upon an innocent girl the sin that is his own burden.

VICTOR
But this monster must die - he is living in glaciers among the mountains. He cannot get food. This horror cannot last, Dr. Waldman

WALDMAN
I'm afraid that this horror is just beginning.
   (Conversation heard as HENRY, AMELIA and
   KATRINA come up the invisible balcony steps)

VICTOR
  (Hands to lips)
Amellia and Henry! Please, father!

  (Enter HENRY and AMELIA and KATRINA
  from balcony)

(HENRY stops in surprise and violent
agitation which he tries to control)

HENRY

Dr. Waldman! So you did come? I'm glad.

WALDMAN

My dear Henry!
(Takes his hand)

AMELIA

Dr. Waldman, do you remember me? I saw you for a moment in Henry's rooms. This is a great compliment, we never supposed you could have spared the time.
(WALDMAN kisses her hand. She senses
tension, looks from one to the other.
Seems about to speak, then hesitates and
says at length)
Is anything wrong?

HENRY

Of course not, darling, what could be wrong?

KATRINA
(After a pause)
Come dear, it's time for you to dress.
(They go out)

HENRY
(Pleading, agitated)
It's most kind of you to come, Dr. Waldman. You HAVE come for the wedding, haven't you? I mean, there isn't any bad news, is there?

WALDMAN

My poor Henry, you know before you ask.

HENRY

He is alive?

WALDMAN

Yes.

HENRY

Fritz said he was dead. I hoped it was true.

WALDMAN

He has become a scourge of God, a terror, a destroyer.

HENRY

But where is he, how does he live, what does he do?

WALDMAN

He lives anywhere, in the mountains, among the glaciers. For good, he preys upon the remote cabins of woodcutters, seizes their beasts, tears them to pieces, and devours them, without fire, like an animal.

HENRY
Did you know this, Victor.

VICTOR
I know - a little.

HENRY
Perhaps then it will live as an animal, die as an animal, never show itself where men and women live ...

WALDMAN
You have not heard the worst.

VICTOR
(Pleads)
He is being married today, and there is nothing he can do NOTHING!

WALDMAN
(Unheeding)
In remote villages beyond Goldstadt, there have been murders.

HENRY
(Aghast)
Murders!

WALDMAN
Committed by someone, of inhuman strength and incredible ferocity. The first one was only two weeks after you left. A legend grew, slowly, of this horror in the mountains. No one believed, at first as only a few peasants had seen. Superstition, the authorities thought. But after the third killing, gendarmes were sent. But what could they do? Scale precipices, live in the eternal snows? He has been seen to go up the overhanging sides of Mount Salove, which no man has ever climbed. This creature's nerves and sinews are of steel, your elixir has given him the strength of ten men. I KNOW. By day and night I prayed for you, Henry. I have talked to the peasants, I have gone to the scenes of some of his crimes.

HENRY
(with hoarse cry)
MY crimes, MINE!

WALDMAN
I wondered whether it could remain an animal, or would it go on developing a MIND? I wondered, but I know, for even at Goldstadt it was leaning fast.

HENRY
Yes. But who could have taught him since that day when he escaped.

                    WALDMAN
Who indeed, when every peasant who has seen him has run in
terror? That I cannot tell you. But he has been learning;
at least he has developed cunning.

                    HENRY
What am I to do?

                    WALDMAN
There is something else.

                    HENRY
There can be nothing worse.

                    WALDMAN
All the early crimes were committed in the mountains beyond
Godstadt, but last week there were two attacks, one half way
between Goldstadt and Belrive, the second ... you must have
heard of it.

                    HENRY
The wood-chopper who was strangled last week near Borck ...
could that have been ... then he's near HERE, can he be coming
to ME?

                    VICTOR
That's absurd. He couldn't possibly know where you live.

                    WALDMAN
Would it not be natural, that the creature should come and
seek out its creator?

                    HENRY
Amelia must never know. He saw Amelia in my rooms. Doctor ...
He was chasing her but she hid from him ...

                    VICTOR
But this is impossible! Since the monster can't talk, ask
questions, or read, then how can he ever learn where you live?

                    WALDMAN
I don't know. Perhaps his movements toward Belrive are
coincidence. But even animals have strange instincts. Can
a cat ask questions, or read, yet cannot a cat find its way ...
home?

                    HENRY
               (With wild laugh)
Home!

                    WALDMAN
               (Sternly)
And have you thought that God might guide him here?

                        HENRY
That's true. I must find him. I can force him to obey. I
am his master.
                        (Before he has finished, FRANKENSTEIN
                        bursts in door, tattered clothes
                        covered with dirt and mud, shaggy hair,
                        they look at him petrified. He has
                        overheard and now, after glaring at them,
                        he suddenly bursts into a mocking laugh,
                        pointing at Henry.

                        FRANKENSTEIN
Master!
                        (Laughs again)
                        (FRANKENSTEIN draws himself up. HENRY
                        threatens to strike him. FRANKENSTEIN
                        raises hands to strangle Henry, VICTOR
                        seizes Henry and pulls him back. HENRY
                        throws Victor off and advances on
                        Frankenstein again)

                        HENRY
What do you want here?

                        FRANKENSTEIN
Wo-man -
                        (HENRY turns away in horror)

                        HENRY
                        (To Waldman)
My power over him is broken.

                        FRANKENSTEIN
                        (Imperiously, to Henry)
The wo-man! Where is the woman?

                        HENRY
There is no woman here.

                        WALDMAN
Frankenstein, mortal woman is not for you.
                        (VICTOR, L. has Baron's gun, which he
                        raises as FRANKENSTEIN, attracted by
                        noise of doves, turns to cage. He
                        watches both doves and men now and
                        then makes clicking imitations sounds
                        during following scene)
In the name of God, I forbid!

                        HENRY
                        (Crossing to Victor)
Give it to me.

WALDMAN
Would you do murder?
(Stands between Frankenstein and them)

HENRY
(Hysterically)
Murder! I told you at Goldstadt, you can't have it both ways, Dr. Waldman, it is murder to kill man, not a monster without a soul.

WALDMAN
You cannot give life, and then take it away -

VICTOR
Then let me do it. It will save the lives of others.

WALDMAN
And get you hanged. Who would believe this story?

VICTOR
(Puts down gun)
We are three against one.

WALDMAN
No, no, you do not know his strength. We must keep him with us, somehow, until he sleeps. Then chains. These murders can be brought home to him, he will be judged mad, confined in an asylum.

VICTOR
Yes, that's the best way.

(FRANKENSTEIN, turning away from cage, remembering, threateningly)

FRANKENSTEIN
Wo-man, my mas-ter!
(Enter BARON L., new, smart coat on. stops amazed seeing Frankenstein)

BARON
(Spluttering)
Who...what...who is this fellow? And my old friend the priest, from Goldstadt.

WALDMAN
I rode over to see my old pupil, Baron

BARON
We're getting him out of your clutches for good, sir, and I think you'll agree that a normal, healthy life at home -
(Looking at Henry)

Henry, what the devil's the matter with you? And who let this
fellow in?
>(Advancing on Frankenstein)

What do you want, fellow?

>FRANKENSTEIN glares at him, does not
>answer, BARON raises his stick.
>FRANKENSTEIN raises his hands in strangu-
>lation gesture, as the others leap forward.

WALDMAN
Baron!

HENRY
Father! You don't understand, this man is our friend!

BARON
>(Lowers stick, turns astonished)

Your friend?

VICTOR
Yes, Baron, at the University, at Goldstadt.

>(BARON looks from Frankenstein to others
>and bursts out into hearty laughter)

BARON
So, and old school-fellow!
>(His instincts of hospitality struggle
>with his amazement and disgust, but he
>manages to speak with fair civility to
>Frankenstein)

Your pardon, sir, I see there has been some mistake. You are
welcome to my house, as a friend of my son.
>(FRANKENSTEIN stares at him, he turns
>away uneasily and impatiently)
>(To Henry)

Well, am I not to have the honor of an introduction?

HENRY
Pardon, Father, this is...that is....

BARON
Well, don't you know his name?
>(To Frankenstein)

What is your name, sir?

FRANKENSTEIN
Fran-ken-stein!

                    BARON

Frankenstein!
          (To Henry)
What the devil does he mean? I ask him his name and he says
Frankenstein...

                    FRANKENSTEIN
          (Suddenly moving about wildly)
Drink, drink!

          (BARON watches him amazed, others anxious.
          FRANKENSTEIN Looks about, sees flowers in
          bowl, takes them from bowl., dashes them on
          floor, picks up bowl, drinks greedily.
          Puts bowl down)

                    BARON
          (Laughs)
Come, sir, no guest in my house drinks water!
          (Takes glass and bottle from tray, pours
          out glass, walks up to Frankenstein, holds
          him out glass with bow, mocking.
          FRANKENSTEIN clumsily takes glass, spilling
          a little, sniffs it suspiciously, drinks it,
          with lightning movement grabs bottle from
          Baron's hand and drinks that down. BARON
          angrily retreats and turns to others.

                    HENRY
          (Involuntary - ejaculation of rebuke)
Frankenstein!

                    BARON
          (Losing temper)
Is this some jest at my expense, gentlemen? Are those the
manners of the young gentlemen at the University, Dr. Waldman?
          (To Frankenstein)
And what the devil do you mean sir, by bellowing out
"Frankenstein" when I ask you who you are? Haven't you got
a tongue in your head?
          (Turning to Henry)
And you, sir, did I hear you call him :Frankenstein" just now?

                    VICTOR
Let me explain, Baron.
          (Speaking quietly)
This poor fellow attached himself to Henry at Goldstadt. He's
a little touched - -
          (Tapping forehead)
People call him Frankenstein's man, so that's why he calls
himself Frankenstein.

                    BARON
Hasn't he got a name?

                    VICTOR
No one knows who he is. He's evidently followed Dr. Waldman
here.

                    BARON
Then I shall thank Dr. Waldman to take him away.
          (Looking at Frankenstein closely)
God, what a monster...He looks as if he'd been dead and
turned half rotten.

          (WALDMAN crosses himself. FRANKENSTEIN
          who has been holding bottle, throws it
          out of window, begins lurching about.)

                    FRANKENSTEIN
Good.
          (Advances on Baron)
More!

                    BARON
Oh, no, my friend, one bottle of THAT drink is more than
sufficient.

                    FRANKENSTEIN
          (Question)
Drink? Drink is ... wa-ter.

                    VICTOR
That was wine!

                    FRANKENSTEIN
          (Fiercely to Baron)
Wine! More wine!
          (A little maudlin, but with commanding
          force to Baron)
Wine!
          (To Henry)
Wo-man!

                    BARON
WOMAN? What does he mean? Where does he think he is? He
may treat my house as a tavern if he likes, but now he's
going a little too far. Wine - wo-man, song, eh, my
beautiful? Come now, you , whatever your name is, you must
clear out of here and go back to Goldstadt. And don't call
yourself Frankenstein, do you hear me? It's my name and my
son's, not yours, and it's an old name too, do you see those
coats of arms up there?
          (Points to escutcheon on wall)
If you haven't got a name, make one up for yourself.

          (FRANKENSTEIN glares at him malevolently
          and advances, BARON withdraws a step.

                    VICTOR
Please, Baron, you mustn't cross him. I'm afraid he's .....
dangerous.

BARON
Dangerous, eh? Well, I fancy there are enough of us here to handle him.

WALDMAN
Baron, believe me, his strength is superhuman.

BARON
Well, I don't want all the furniture smashed and the girls upset, but what in God's name are we going to do with him?

FRANKENSTEIN
(With sudden cry)
Where is the woman

BARON
(In rage)
How dare you?
(Rushes at him - General scuffle.)
FRANKENSTEIN looks about him cunningly, pauses, as though making up his mind, then turns and rushes out R.)

VICTOR
Come, come, we must not lose sight of him!
(HENRY, VICTOR and WALDMAN go out hurriedly, R. Enter KATRINA, L.)

KATRINA
Father! What's all the noise about?

BARON
Some creature followed that old priest here - they say he's a little gone in the head and that he attached himself to Henry, at Goldstadt. Apparently at that university they breed not only mad professors and atheists, but idiots as well. Nearly knocked me over. They've run out to catch him.

KATRINA
(She is untying boxes, removes wedding wreath from one)
Oh, poor fellow. What will they do to him?

BARON
Lock him up until after the wedding, I suppose. I'd better help them. Don't let our bride see him, she might get nerves.

KATRINA
(Laughs)
Oh, but don't you remember the old legend father, that an idiot at a wedding brings good luck?

(BARON GOES OFF, KATRINA, following)
(FRANKENSTEIN appears, climbing over balcony. Searches room with swift motions like a panther, finally stops before cage of doves. Is interested again, looks from them to birds outside

     in sky, roughly pulls open door, takes
     one (the artificial one), carries it to
     balcony, crushing it in great hands
     throws it in the air)

       FRANKENSTEIN

Fly, bird, fly, fly!
     (To his astonishment it falls.
     Pointing down)
Bird fall! Water Shining water!
     (Turns gazes puzzled at birds in cage.
     Enter KATRINA, who goes up to him and
     touches his arm gentle. After pause
     wonderingly)
You ... not fear?

       KATRINA

Who are you?

       FRANKENSTEIN

Frank-en-stein.

       KATRINA
     (Misunderstanding)
Yes, that is our name. You didn't mean to frighten them.

       FRANKENSTEIN

Frighten? Fear?

I knew that! Why have you come to us?

       FRANKENSTEIN

Mas-ter...

       KATRINA

Master? Do you mean Henry, my brother?

       FRANKENSTEIN

Man ... mas-ter...not mas-ter now.
     (Draws himself up, half-laughing, raising
     hands in strangling motion. Wonderingly
     as she does not show terror
All men fear...
     (Touches his breast)

       KATRINA

Why should I fear you?

       FRANKENSTEIN

Other wo-man fear...

KATRINA
What other woman -- Amelia? Have you seen her?

FRANKENSTEIN
(Nods)
Yes. Above. At window.

KATRINA
(In distress)
Oh, dear! Did she see you?

FRANKENSTEIN
No. Frankenstein hide -- out there --
(Vague gesture towards the outdoors)

KATRINA
She mustn't see you. She'd be frightened. If I could only make you understand.

FRANKENSTEIN
Frighten -- all people frightened -- not you. Why - why other woman fear?

KATRINA
I can't make you understand. Oh, dear, I'm sorry.

FRANKENSTEIN
Sorry?

KATRINA
Don't you even know what sorry means?
(He shakes his head)
Oh, dear, how can I explain it to you?
(Impulsively she holds out her hand to him. He touches it wonderingly, then holds it, then takes both hands, while he talks)

FRANKENSTEIN
No man touch Frankenstein - fear. Hit Frankenstein. Master beat - not now. I kill! You woman, you not hate?
(She shakes her head, then gives a little scream. He had unconsciously crushed her hands. She holds her hands together and cries a little without a handkerchief, like a child)
(Agitated)
Why? Why?
(He is in distress, doesn't know what to do. Lumbering gets down on knee.

KATRINA
It's all right. You hurt my hands a little. You didn't mean to. You see you are so strong, you don't know when you hurt.

FRANKENSTEIN
(Complete self abasement)
Frankenstein hurt - Frankenstein hurt --
(Unconsciously his hands go to his eyes,

> he stops, looking wonderingly at one
> hand)

KATRINA

You're crying too.

FRANKENSTEIN

Crying -- these crying?

KATRINA
> (Wiping her eyes)

Those are tears. I was silly, it didn't hurt very much, not enough to cry about.

FRANKENSTEIN

Tears.

KATRINA
> (Laughs suddenly)

But now you know what sorry means. You were sorry - just now when you hurt my hands. That's why you cried.
> (FRANKENSTEIN jumps up, laughing also)

Why, you were really like a little boy, just now. Why do you say people hate you?

FRANKENSTEIN

Hate Frankenstein. All people. Hurt Frankenstein.

KATRINA

But I don't, my poor friend.

FRANKENSTEIN

Friend?

KATRINA

Don't you know what friend is either? Somebody one's fond of. I should like to help you.

FRANKENSTEIN

You woman, you beauty like...like garden. Like sky. Not pain like...other woman.

KATRINA

I don't understand you.

FRANKENSTEIN
> (He is almost on his knees)

Help Frankenstein.

KATRINA

Of course, I will. If only you could go away a little while, just until after the wedding.

FRANKENSTEIN

Wedding?

KATRINA
Yes, Henry's wedding. Didn't you know? My brother, your friend, he's going to marry Amelia.

FRANKENSTEIN
Marry?   Other woman?   Mate?

KATRINA
Yes.

FRANKENSTEIN
(Savagely)
No.

KATRINA
Yes, today.

FRANKENSTEIN
No!   No!   No!

KATRINA
In an hour! That's why you -

FRANKENSTEIN
No! Frankenstein master now. Frankenstein mate. Frankenstein woman.
(As he moves about KATRINA suddenly sees cage)

KATRINA
(With little cry)
Oh, my dove! How did it get out?
(She runs to cage. To Frankenstein)
There were three, the cage door was shut.
(FRANKENSTEIN points to cage, points outside)
I see, you took it, you let it fly. You wanted to be kind, but I'm afraid some wild bird will kill it.

FRANKENSTEIN
(Walking to balcony)
Not fly.
(Points down)

KATRINA
It fell down?

FRANKENSTEIN
(Looking)
Wa-ter...shin-ing wa-ter.

KATRINA
Did it drown?
(He stares dumbly at her)
I mean, did it go under the water? Poor dove! You must have crushed it. Your hands are so strong.
(He looks miserable)
It's all right, I know you didn't mean to, only -

FRANKENSTEIN
(With lateral motions of hands, conveys
picture of dove floating)
On water. Like leaves. Beauty. Shining water.

KATRINA
On water. Poor dove.
(She runs out to balcony, looks over
comes back)
I can't see it. Oh!
(She goes towards him, seeing his
distress)
Don't look so sad. You didn't mean to.

FRANKENSTEIN
Frankenstein hurt - hurt dove, hurt friend.

KATRINA
You mean my hands? Never mind, they don't hurt now.

FRANKENSTEIN
Tears. Pain.
(Turns again, looks down from balcony)
Bird - wa-ter -
(Repeats floating gesture)
That beau-ty too.

KATRINA
You saw it floating. Perhaps it's not dead but only hurt.

FRANKENSTEIN
Hurt.

KATRINA
Perhaps I could find it - -
(Goes towards balcony and stops)
Where did it fall?
(He makes vague downward gesture)
You must come with me, down to the lake.
(Half distracted)
Come. Don't you understand? I cannot leave you here. Amelia is putting on her wedding gown, she's coming down here any moment. She mustn't see you - if she's frightened of you. And if the men come back and find you here - - there'll be a lot of noise.

FRANKENSTEIN
(Wondering)
Frankenstein .. with you?

KATRINA
(Holds out her hand with a smile)
Yes, of course. We'll find my dove and then you must stay away until after the wedding.
(As they go off)
See, there's my boat, we'll take that, it can't have floated far.

(She walks along the balcony out of site)

        FRANKENSTEIN
    (Looks down at lake)
Wa-ter ... bird ... beau-ty ...friend.
    (EXIT FRANKENSTEIN, following Katrina)

    (FRITZ enters from L. before they are
    out of sight. A moment's terror at sight
    of Frankenstein. Then he slips over to
    door, watches, finally locks over balcony.
    Suddenly makes motions of protest, which
    grow more excited at what he sees. Tries
    to call out and cannot. Finally rushes
    after them.

    (BARON marshals in WALDMAN and VICTOR, R.
    talking as they enter. He is in a jovial
    mood, laughing and amused by the adventure)

          BARON
No, no, no I won't have you wandering all about the place
looking behind every boulder, like that mad son of mine.
Where the devil is Henry now, and what sort of stories
do you think will get about the neighborhood? Do you suppose
I want all Belrive to think that an escaped lunatic has
terrified me and my whole household.
    (goes to door L., calls loudly)
Amelia! Katrina!

         AMELIA'S VOICE
Yes, Baron.
    (VICTOR and WALDMAN look at each other,
     disturbed)

          BARON
    (Crosses and calls, R.)
Helene! Where the devil is everybody? Helene!
    (Pause, he calls to her as he sees her,
     off)
Bring more wine and some glasses!
    (Turns to them)
Can't you see what's happened? Your pet maniac has had enough
of us and has gone back to your abode of the higher learning,
Dr. Waldman, where you'll find him when you get there.
And scaring all the peasants out of their wits along the road.
I must say I'd rather you had him on your hands than me.
    (HELENE enters with tray, puts it down
     exits. BARON pours out three glasses)
Thanks, Helene, now go find Master Henry. One last glass to
toast the bridegroom before we leave.
    (BARON and VICTOR drink - WALDMAN pretends
     to)
Tell me, Dr. Waldman, what do you thin of our Henry now we've
got him away from the University?

                    WALDMAN

He looks much better, Baron.

                    BARON

Better!

                    WALDMAN

He was suffering from overwork.

                    BARON
              (Explosively)
Overwork! I think you're all mad, over there in Goldstadt.
Do people faint from overwork? There he was, in a dead
faint on the floor of his lodgings. And in comes Amelia
in hysterics, with Victor. Well, the plain uneducated country-
man put them all in the carriage and drove straight back
here to Belrive.

                    WALDMAN
              (With great effort)
Baron, about this marriage -

              (FRITZ rushes in, stops, makes wild
               gestures at them. BARON turns on him
               furiously)

                    BARON
What the hell are you doing gin here? I sent you down to the
stables. Get out of here.
          FRITZ rushes out R.)
Another one of your lunatics from Goldstadt, Doctor! Yes,
what about this marriage? Where is the bridegroom? We
must be down in the village in less than an hour. A simple
country wedding. Doctor, just our own parish priest, a few
neighbors, the village people and the tenants...you must
stay and lend some ecclesiastical reinforcement.
          VICTOR gets up restlessly)
What's the matter with you, boy?

                    VICTOR
Nothing, Baron, nothing at all; that creature upset me a
little, perhaps.

                    BARON
Good God, I should think he had. You too, Dr. Waldman,
you might be a pair of mourners at a funeral. Come, another
glass, Father.

                    WALDMAN
No thank you.

                    BARON
Victor?
          (VICTOR shakes his head)
Thank you. I think I'll go and find Fritz - -

BARON
(pours himself more wine)
You'd better go and find Katrina and see if the girls are ready. These women take so much time over last minute -

VICTOR
(Alarmed)
Where is Katrina?

BARON
She started out with me, then came back. She thought Amelia might be frightened.

(VICTOR starts out L door, stops as
MAID crosses stage quickly from R.
to balcony followed by FRITZ)

MAID
(in great alarm)
Oh, master, master. Fritz made me look from the cellar window. I think I saw him - with something white -
(What she sees from balcony makes her recoil
horrified with scram. She retreats into room)

BARON
What's the matter?
(Enter FRANKENSTEIN from balcony carrying
the drowned KATRINA, her body dripping
water. He steps into the room, stands
looking about him, bewildered, dazed.
The men rush up to him, VICTOR pulls out
couch, they take body and put it down.
WALDMAN kneels by body, testing it for
sign of life, crosses himself)
Oh God, no - not that! Oh, my child!

WALDMAN
Go to your mistress, don't let her come in.

(Exit MAID, L. crying)
(To Fritz)
Go find your master.
(Exit FRITZ, R.)

VICTOR
There is no use asking him now. We must get Henry, at once.

BARON
I must go to the Church - to my wife - my poor wife - -
    (Exit Baron, R.)

    (Enter HENRY, running R., almost colliding with
    Baron as he comes in. FRITZ comes behind him -
    watches - crouched in far corner of room R.)

HENRY
I saw him with Katrina in his arms, what has he done to her, what has he done to her?
    (Flings himself by body. FRANKENSTEIN stands
    dumbly begins to cry. HENRY looks up)
Is she dead?

WALDMAN
The heart has stopped.

VICTOR
You made a dead heart beat. You brought a man to life when he'd been killed - -

HENRY
    (Hysterical, but hopeful)
Katrina. Katrina! Have I been given this knowledge to save your life - -
    (Pushes her hair back, puts arms
    under her to lift her)
We must take her at once to Goldstadt, my machines, my elixir - everything is there.

VICTOR
Thank God, the coach is ready.

    (As they lift her, her head drops
    back sharply)

HENRY
Her throat - look! He's strangled her.
    (They lay her down, he feels around
    her neck)
    (Silence)
Her neck is broken. I can do nothing.

VICTOR
Why not? You've done it before. That man who was hanged.

HENRY
Strangulation defeated me. I told you that. When the bones of the neck are broken, the chain of nerves from the brain down to the spine and to the rest of the body is broken too. I could make her heart beat - -

VICTOR
Do that - do something. Don't give up.

HENRY
It would be only a muscle contracting and expanding. The brain would remain dead.
     (Stands up)

VICTOR
     (Half hysterical)
Then what good is this knowledge, this power that you were so proud - - -

HENRY
It is a power of evil. You warned me. Dr. Waldman and in my mad presumption I would not listen. You, I was proud - you reminded me that pride was the sin of the fallen angel. I tried to create, I tried to make myself God's equal. This is his answer.

VICTOR
     (To Frankenstein)
How did this happen?

FRANKENSTEIN
She not speak...why?

HENRY
     (looking up - dull, flat voice)
Why did you do this to her?

     (WALDMAN turns away, kneels by corpse
      in prayer)

FRANKENSTEIN
She touched...hand - -
     (Holds out hand)
we go ... wa-ter...

VICTOR
You were in the boat with her?

FRANKENSTEIN

     (nods head)
     (Makes motion of pushing)
Boat float...like laves..like bird...shin-ing in wa-ter...
     (With gesture of picker her up)
She beau-ty. I want her float - on shin-ing wa-ter...she not blot. Cry. Not speak.

HENRY
Murderer, You killed my sister.

FRANKENSTEIN
Kill? No, this kill!
     (Bringing up his hands in gesture of strangling)

VICTOR
Yes, you strangled her, with your hands, and then you drowned her.

FRANKENSTEIN
She say - -hands too strong. She not speak - never speak?

VICTOR
She's dead. Dead!

(WALDMAN rises)

FRANKENSTEIN
Dead? Fran-ken-stein...kill - friend?
        (Wildly appealing to Waldman)
Hurt...hurt...pain...
        (Hand to head)
Not tell me shin-ing wa-ter kill. She touch....she not hate me-
        (Breaking down with wild sobs
         sinks beside body)

        (HENRY crosses to gun, takes it up.
        WALDMAN follows, slight struggle.
        VICTOR joins. The two force gun
        away from Henry - - WALDMAN unloads
        it and throws cartridges out over
        balcony)

VICTOR
He didn't know.

WALDMAN
        (Sternly)
Vengeance is Mind, saith the Lord.

HENRY
Yes, but why her, her? Why not me, it was my sin! I am the one who should be punished!

WALDMAN
You are being punished, my son.

HENRY
        (Rushing at Frankenstein...kicks him
         strikes him)
Get away from her, you devil.

WALDMAN
        (To Victor)
Take her to her room. Leave me alone with him.

VICTOR
We can't do that, Dr. Waldman.

HENRY
Go, go, it was God who sent this thing to find me here - this thing that I let loose upon the world. You would not let me kill him, then let him kill me!

> (FRANKENSTEIN scrambles up from floor, snarls at Henry)

FRANKENSTEIN
I...kill mas-ter!

HENRY
(To Waldman)
It's not his murder, it's mine! Take her away, for God's sake, take her away. Take her to her room.

> (WALDMAN and VICTOR pick up body and carry it off L.)

HENRY
Go to Amelia, Dr. Waldman. But tell her it was an accident.

> (FRANKENSTEIN makes few steps after body dashing tears from eyes)

FRANKENSTEIN
(To himself)
Kill...kill beau-ty...kill friend. Why did you not tell me shining water could kill?

> (In following scene HENRY has to drag out of Frankenstein to content of his mind because Frankenstein can't talk, but Frankenstein shows that he understands most of what is said to him)

HENRY
Frankenstein!

FRANKENSTEIN
(Forgetting Katrina, sidles up to him. menacingly, speaks with savage irony)
Mas-ter! Frank-en-stein find mas-ter)

HENRY
How have you found me? How did you know?
> (FRANKENSTEIN gives a horrid laugh)

That doesn't matter now. What do you want?

FRANKENSTEIN
Find Mas-ter...find the wo-man.

HENRY
(wildly)
Every woman would flee from you in horror, except my sister whom you murdered.

                    FRANKENSTEIN
Fran-ken-stein saw..wo-man above - up there.

                    HENRY
That woman is not for you - there can be no woman for you.

                    FRANKENSTEIN
Man...woman. Man...mate.

                    HENRY
But you're not a man. Don't you understand that?
          (FRANKENSTEIN nods)
You know!

                    FRANKENSTEIN
          (Pointing accusing finger)
You...you...
          (With other hand taps his breast)

                    HENRY
          (Hysterically)
Yes, you know! God gave life to all men, but I, a man, gave
life to you! How can you know this?
          (FRANKENSTEIN with triumphant laugh, takes papers
             from picket, hands them to Henry. Takes them
             looks at them)
My notes. That - that's my coat. You went back, you stole
my clothes, you found these papers - the notes of my experiments, my dissecting, my filthy work -
          (Pause, FRANKENSTEIN looks at him)
But you have learned to read - you understand what I did

          (FRANKENSTEIN shakes head)

          (VICTOR returns -- says aside to Henry:
           "She wants to come. I told her not to."
           Henry nods)
How do you know what those notes are?

                    FRANKENSTEIN
Man read...man make Fran-ken-stein know.

                    HENRY
Who was it? What man read my notes?

                    FRANKENSTEIN
Man in field - I make him tell.
          (Gesture of hands to throat)

                    HENRY
Then my secret is known. Who was he? Where did he go?
          (FRANKENSTEIN makes gesture of throttling
             something, and then tossing it aside)
          (Understanding)
After he told you, you killed him?

(FRANKENSTEIN gurgles and chuckles assent)
(Looking at papers)

A letter from Amelia -
(looking at it)

It speaks of our house at Belrive. Then the man told you where I live, how to get here, before you killed him!
(FRANKENSTEIN nods)
(Jamming papers in pocket)

Why do you commit these crimes? Even a beast kills only for food...

FRANKENSTEIN

Hate!

VICTOR

What do you mean?

FRANKENSTEIN

Men hate -
(Beating breast)

I hate men.

HENRY

You needn't hate men, hate me, it is I whom you should kill. But if all men flee from you except those you killed, how have you learned to understand so much? You filthy mass that moves and talks, who taught you?

FRANKENSTEIN

I learn...I know...man, wo-man, lit-tle men -
(Indicating children by holding out hand
to show their height)

Man...find...high up...moun-tain...house. They not see... I see, I hear.

HENRY

But how could you see and hear, if they didn't see you?

FRANKENSTEIN

Fran-ken-stein...out.   Man - wo-man - in - not see.

VICTOR

I can't understand you.

(FRANKENSTEIN lies down on floor, show
by pantomime looking through hole in
wall, then puts ear to wall)

HENRY

I understand. But how could you learn so much?

FRANKENSTEIN

(Getting up)

Great fire come...great fire go.
(Holds out hands, ticks off his fingers
many times, twelve or fifteen, in effort
to count, then stops)

HENRY

For weeks you watched. You heard these people, who didn't suspect the horror that was listening, talking about their daily life, you saw how men eat and sleep, ideas came to you -
        (FRANKENSTEIN picks up book from table,
         opens it, looks at it)
Yes, you saw a man reading.

FRANKENSTEIN

Man looked...spoke words...after great fire go...then sleep.

HENRY

You heard a man reading the Bible to his family....

FRANKENSTEIN
       (Nods)
Prayer. Who is God?

HENRY

You never could understand, He's a man's God, not a God of beasts. I made your life - I am your God, Frankenstein.

FRANKENSTEIN

You my God!
       (After a pause FRANKENSTEIN indicates by
       bending of hands to eyes, but without
       getting down to floor, his looking
       through into hut)
I saw man...wo-man...man...mate, bed. You Fran-ken-stein's God... Frank-en-stein in pray - God give mate.

HENRY

You - pray to me! I hate you and yet I made you, you are mine, you are part of me. I knew how God felt When He made man, and man turned out a filthy mess. He must have hated us and yet... we were His responsibility.

FRANKENSTEIN

Man...mate. Fran-ken-stein...al-one.

HENRY

But I can't give you a mate.

FRANKENSTEIN

Make me mate.

HENRY

No.

FRANKENSTEIN

Then I kill.

HENRY
(Laughs wildly)
Kill, that's what I want you to do. Kill me! What have I got left? You've killed my sister - - that's practically killing my mother and father. Do you think I can marry Amelia now? Kill me, that's what I want!
(Goes up to Frankenstein, who makes motions of strangling, then stops-- looks cunning)

FRANKENSTEIN

Kill first, then take your wo-man.

VICTOR

Good God! have you thought of that?

HENRY

She's not here.

FRANKENSTEIN

Yes, here. Frankenstein saw her...

HENRY

And if I do - - what you say....

FRANKENSTEIN

Then I take mate...go away men who hate...mountains...sweep leaves...No hate....not kill you....not kill men.

HENRY

If I do this...you will go away now, keep away from Amelia from that woman
(FRANKENSTEIN nods)
You will go away now?
(FRANKENSTEIN nods cunningly)

FRANKENSTEIN

Go with master. Watch Master.

HENRY

Victor, I must do it, if it will save her. It will take months! And I might not succeed again.

FRANKENSTEIN

Then I kill.

HENRY

I can't work any more in Goldstadt, I must get my -
(To Victor)

God, that charnel house of mine at Goldstadt! Where is the formula?
>   (Searches through papers - taken from
>   Frankenstein's pocket, finds what he wants)

I must go up into the mountains -

>   (FRANKENSTEIN nods)

FRANKENSTEIN

You go get horses now.

VICTOR

My God you can't do it again.

HENRY

All I can do is to get him away from here - to the mountains. Get me that gun.
>   (VICTOR slips it to him)

I have cartridges at Goldstadt. In the mountains I can kill him - shoot him - poison - somehow!

FRANKENSTEIN

Go!
>   (HENRY staggers. VICTOR throws arm
>   around him to support him)

You on horse - I follow!

>   (FRANKENSTEIN goes out on balcony,
>   begins to climb rail - almost disappears)

HENRY

Amelia -

VICTOR

Dr. Waldman is with her.

>   (They go out. FRANKENSTEIN appears on balcony,
>   as FRITZ comes out from his corner. Seeing
>   FRANKENSTEIN, he ducks in terror behind couch.
>   FRANKENSTEIN waits a second, then gently slides
>   door shut and locks it, starts for door L.
>   FRITZ runs after him, leaps, catching Franken-
>   stein's legs to stop him. FRANKENSTEIN picks
>   him up, gives quick twist and contemptuously
>   tosses him over Balcony.)
>   (AMELIA'S voice heard calling, "Henry".
>   FRANKENSTEIN waits, crouched, half hidden from
>   door L. which she enters, door closing behind
>   her. She is in bridal dress and veil, without
>   wreath, weeping. Starts for balcony calling:
>   Henry, where are you going?" Meets Frankenstein
>   and jumps back, too terrified to scream.)

FRANKENSTEIN
Woman!

AMELIA
You! What do you want here?

FRANKENSTEIN
You! Woman

AMELIA
No!
> (Tries to reach balcony, calling "Henry".
> He catches and holds her back.

FRANKENSTEIN
Master gone - away.

AMELIA
I know, I saw him. Let me go, I must call him.

FRANKENSTEIN
No!

AMELIA
Then you must go after him. Please - please. Go quickly and bring him back.
> (He stands quietly, still holding her)

No mustn't go. He doesn't know what he's doing. He can't leave his mother and father now! Oh, don't you see, Katrina's dead. - - -
> (His hands drop, and she jumps back free,
> but unable to move by the horror of her
> discover)

You - - -they said it was an accident. Did you drown Katrina?

FRANKENSTEIN
> (In grief, covers face with hands)

I - did not know.

AMELIA
But why - why? I don't understand! Why is Henry running away?

FRANKENSTEIN
Send him away!

AMELIA
You're the - the thing he said he'd made. I never believed him. It - it isn't possible.
> (He makes a motion toward her. She leaps
> against the back of the couch, fascinated
> like a bird before a snake)

It isn't possible -
> (Her voice has become husky from fear)

Who are you?

FRANKENSTEIN
            (Draws himself up arrogantly)
I - I Frankenstein master. Send him away.
            (Suddenly - almost humble)
Wait...for you -
            (She tries to run, but he seizes her
            She screams: "Victor, help!" In the
            struggle he tears off her bridal veil
            and the top of her dress - - pulls her
            part way down on couch)

AMELIA
No, no! Go away. Can't you see you disgust me - you fill
me with horror.
            (Staring up at him in terror)
It's true. You're not human.

FRANKENSTEIN
            (Pleading)
Not horror. Not hate. Frankenstein love - -want - -

AMELIA
You can't love - - you're not human. You're Henry's evil
spirit, his devil. You're not human! You can't do this - -
            (With a sudden scream)
Help! Victor, help!

            (between her screams can be heard his
            whinings and pleading "woman" - "mate" -
            "Frankenstein, mate". Then Victor's
            voice calling, "Amelia", in answer to her
            screams. Someone shakes the locked door R.,
            VICTOR'S VOICE CALLS again; "Amelia, let
            me in."

            (AMELIA tears herself away, half dressed
            and flees through door L. FRANKENSTEIN
            stands half in stupor. VICTOR again shakes
            door. Sound of feet on stairs above, and
            slamming door. FRANKENSTEIN rushes out L.,
            sound of heavy feet on stairs and of smashing
            blows at door above. At this point VICTOR
            rushes in balcony window and across to door L.
            and BARON can be heard knocking and shaking
            the locked door R. as)

            THE CURTAIN FALLS

ACT III

Six months later, A hut in the Jura mountains, bare and rough in appearance. There is a large double window waist high in the rear wall, through which are seen mountains and moonlight, later obscured by clouds and lit up by flashes of lightning.

Door L. and R. Right one, backstage, leads into hallway. The other, left front, into Henry's bedroom.

Rough table and two stools L., a lamp on the table, closed chest R. Brazier in which charcoal fire glows R., a number of bottles, papers, retorts, etc. on table. Against the wall R., place crossways, is a low couch or bier on which lies an inanimate form covered by drapery. The same electric machine in shadows against back wall, left.

The CURTAIN discovers HENRY working over a liquid in a retort on the table. He is in rags, long tangled hair, emaciated, at last stages of exhausttion.

He stagger to chest R., takes out papers, returns to table, adds few drops from bottle to elixir in retort, goes back, replaces papers in chest. Then comes to table again and tries to go on working, but sinks on stool, head in hands, then staggers to feet with exhaustion and drags himself into his bedroom through door L. front.

FRANKENSTEIN looks through rear windows. Not seeing Henry he shakes windows in rage, then disappears, and crash is heard of R. as of outer door being forced. FRANKENSTEIN enters through door R. rear. His hair is longer, his appearance even more frightful than in preceding acts, the same clothes as he wore in Act II, but much torn and ragged. He looks about Utters inarticulate sounds of anger. Goes to form on bier, lifts corner of sheet, looks, makes inarticulate noises. (The audience at no time sees the figure). Roams about room, pick-

G

                          ing up bottles, etc. Then goes off
                          L. into Henry's room, drags Henry
                          back on stage, points to retort and
                          bottles on table, and to covered form.

                    HENRY

Do you want to kill me before I've don it? I'm merely a man. I'm not like you. I must sleep sometimes. I thought you were a dream, another one of my filthy dreams!
            (Sinks on stool)

                    FRANKENSTEIN
            (In tone of menace and command)
Work!

                    HENRY
            (Hysterically)
Get out. I must have rest, I'm exhausted, I can't go on.

                    FRANKENSTEIN
            (Near corpse, makes vague gestures
              over it)
To-night!

                    HENRY

To-night! You're more insane than usual. It's brilliant moonlight.

                    FRANKENSTEIN
No Look!
            (Points out window, moonlight is
              fading, clouds seen)
Storm - big storm - coming.

          HENRY get up and goes to window)

                    HENRY
You're right. But it won't break for an hour. Give me an hour's rest.
            (Screams at him)
I must have rest. My nerves must be steady - - -

                    FRANKENSTEIN
Storm come soon. Machine live then -
            (Points to bier)
her live. Tonight - her - mate - we go -

            (Faint thunder)

                    HENRY
Yes, go with her, forever. You swore it. Away from me, away from all mankind.
            (FRANKENSTEIN nods)
All right, demon.
            (Starts tinkering with vials on table,
            goes to chest, takes out bottle, drinks)

FRANKENSTEIN
(Advancing on him)
Drink!
(Snarling, starts to take bottle, HENRY
pours out remainder of contents on floor
throws bottle in corner, FRANKENSTEIN
snarls at him, raises hands in strangling
motion)

HENRY
(Laughs)
Go, Kill me! I wish you would, before I do this thing -

FRANKENTEIN drops hands)

FRANKENSTEIN
Then I take woman -
(Sky quite dark. Faint lightning and thunder)

HENRY
(Sullenly)
Get out and I will finish. Then I shall be free, no more your slave.
(FRANKENSTEIN shambles towards door
R. rear, pauses)

FRANKENSTEIN
Fran-ken-stein watch!

HENRY
You always watch. When I tried to escape you dragged me back, you tracked me down like a blood-hound --

FRANKENSTEIN
(Chuckles)
When you tired kill, I took away gun.
(Pausing near body)
No more...a-lone, her ... no hate ...no hor-ror.
(Draws himself up threateningly, pointing)
WORK!

(Exits.

(HENRY follows him off, can be heard shutting
outer door - re-enters, examines liquid in
retort, fusses with wires of machine which
fizzles and gives off light as before, only more
quietly, when lightning is seen. Goes to
chest again, opens it, but as he is taking
out paper there is a rap at the window)

3-4

>   (HENRY starts violently, goes to window,
>   sees DR. WALDMAN'S face, indicates by
>   sign he is to go to door. Holds up
>   light as he goes toward door, which opens.
>   In rushes AMELIA, followed by WALDMAN
>   and VICTOR -- all cloaked. Her hair blown
>   by wind, all exhausted and excited.

> (PAUSE)

                        HENRY
Are you ghosts?

                        AMELIA
Henry! Henry!
>   (Goes to him, but draws back, she
>   cannot embrace him. WALDMAN takes
>   one hand, VICTOR throws an arm around
>   him)

                        HENRY
My friends. My friends.
>   (almost weeping)
How did you find me?

                        AMELIA
Henry, Poor Henry. We searched everywhere. It was the
Doctor who finally ---

                        WALDMAN
No, it was Amelia. She never let us rest.

                        AMELIA
Poor Henry. Poor Henry. We went to Goldstadt to find you after
we buried Katrina.

                        WALDMAN
I rode there at once. But you had already gone. So I returned
to Belrive --

                        HENRY
You were at Katrina's funeral, then?

                        WALDMAN
Yes. And the next day we all went back to Godstadt.

                        AMELIA
Your books and all your instruments had disappeared
during those three days, so I guessed ---

                        HENRY
What?

                        AMELIA
Your reason for going away. Then I made Victor tell me.

                        VICTOR
Your parents thought you were out of your mind with grief.

HENRY
Poor mother -- She must have been nearly out of hers.

WALDMAN
Your father too.

HENRY
I'm afraid to ask news of them.

WALDMAN
Your father had gendarmes searching for months. Then your mother broke down, and we persuaded him to take her away for awhile.

AMELIA
But we never stopped searching.
(Storm grows louder)

HENRY
How did you find me? I thought this was the loneliest spot in the Jura Mountains.

WALDMAN
The peasants won't talk to the gendarmes. But I heard tales. One day I went to the peak above the village where Fritz thought he had seen the monster.

HENRY
At lest I have spared Fritz this horror.

WALDMAN
Yes, he has been spared - a lot. In that village I heard of a strange young man who had staggered up this mountain with a sack of books - a mad student they thought. And of another man --

HENRY
Had they seen him. He only goes away from here at night.

WALDMAN
Herdsmen had seene him from other mountain peaks. Cattle and sheep have disappeared.

HENRY
There have been no tales of murders?

WALDMAN
No.

HENRY
Of course he steals, for he has been bringing me food. He is my willing slave again. He carried up my books and my machine. He has even tried to help. But he watches me, day and night.

(Lightening the machine fizzes and spits:
they turn in horror to look at it)

VICTOR
Henry, what are you doing?

HENRY

It doesn't matter now.
>(He is holding tightly to one of
>Amelia's hands)

It is so good to see you. I feel sane again. I have been mad, for months.

AMELIA

Poor Henry. Who wouldn't be?

HENRY

But how did you come? Even with Frankenstein's help it took me three days to get here.

WALDMAN

When I was sure, I told them. We took horses at dawn -- We climbed all day until the horses gave out. There's a herdsman hut a few miles below here --

HENRY

Old Peter, I've seen him sometimes from a distance. He's a lunatic too, like me. But harmless.

AMELIA

Henry, don't talk so

HENRY

...but a cripple, so he can't climb up here.

AMELIA

Henry, when -- that machine was gone and your books, I know what you were doing, and that you were doing it for me - for my safety. So I made Victor bring me.

HENRY

Why?

AMELIA

Because, if -- if it is me he wants, I'd rather --I'd rather he had his way --
>(From HENRY and VICTOR At once "No")

than you should do again --make again --
>(Gesture toward bier)

commit that sin over again.

HENRY

Is that why you came?

AMELIA

Yes.

VICTOR

My God, Amelia, you did not tell me this.
>(To Henry)

I'd never have brought her.

AMELIA

Don't you see, Henry -- you can't - people the world with a race of monsters like him.

HENRY
What else can I do--but bring this thing to life? I've tried to escape; he catches me, and then tortures me--
(shows scars on arms)
I've tried to make him kill me, he tells me of the crimes he'll commit and of--My God, if he comes back and sees you here! Get back there - by the door, out of sight of the windows.
(Pushes her toward bedroom door)
I've tried to kill him--he breaks my traps and laughs at me, he took my gun, he carries my knife. He sleeps in some place I cannot find--if he sleeps at all. He never eats food near here, for I have also tried poison. He is always watching.

AMELIA
Henry, poor Henry!

HENRY
Having committed one crime, Dr. Waldman, I have no choice but to commit another, perhaps a worse crime. Tonight!

WALDMAN
What do you mean?

HENRY
Amelia has told you--there is the woman; I promised her to him tonight. You saw my first experiment, when I was filled with pride and elation. No, on another night almost like that, with only despair and horror in my heart--

(Breaks down. AMELIA soothes him)

WALDMAN
(simply)
It was God that guided us up here tonight.

HENRY
For what? To see the finish of my work? For now I must complete it--he'll find you, he'll kill us--and then--Amelia---

AMELIA
It is better than--to set loose on the world a race of -Frankensteins.

(A howl outside)

HENRY
Oh God, why did you come? Victor, you'll help me - take Amelia in there, that is my bedroom. Stay there with her, the shutters are barred, he can only enter it through here. He must know someone is with me.

(Exit AMELIA reluctantly, and VICTOR)

WALDMAN
Will your damn your soul to an eternal Hell?

                    HENRY
What does my soul matter now? I must save her - - all of you.
Oh, don't you see? There is no other way.
            (Tales bottle of fluid, holds it over
             test tubes)
You shall see the last rite - - - or it is the first? Look!
            (Pours one colorless fluid into another
             colorless one, they turn a bright color.
             Holds up tube.
My elixir!
            (Flashes and thunder and FRANKENSTEIN'S
             face through the window)

                    WALDMAN
My son, you are Satan, the Anti-Christ!

                    HENRY
I have become so.

                    WALDMAN
Suppose you fail? You say he will kill us all and take Amellia.
Suppose you succeed? Will he keep his word to you, and go
away - with his mate - and live quietly, doing no harm?

                    HENRY
I do not know. It is my only chance - - Amelia's only chance - -

            (FRANKENSTEIN bursts in through window
             shattering of glass - - more lightning)

                    FRANKENSTEIN
The woman is here. The woman - -

                    HENRY
There is your woman -
            (Points to bier)

                    FRANKENSTEIN
No, Not now. The woman - - in there - -
            (Starts toward door. WALDMAN places
             himself before it.)

                    HENRY
Your oath to go away - tonight!

                    FRANKENSTEIN
Oath! You say - not kill - always try kill Frankenstein-

                    HENRY
Your promise - -
            (FRANKENSTEIN, thrusting aside Waldman is
             about to enter door. HENRY raises hand with
             elixir in it, pours it on brazier. Sharp sudden flash.
I'll break my promise too!

3-9

> (Tears up formula, throws bits away. Picks
> up a heavy bar, smashes at machine.
> FRANKENSTEIN leaps at him, throws him over
> table, struggle, one quick twist, and he
> throws him to the floor - dead, then out
> the window)

> (WALDMAN kneels, prays, holding crucifix.
> AMELIA and VICTOR have rushed in -- AMELIA
> clings to Victor. Suddenly FRANKENSTEIN
> throws himself down by window, sobbing)

FRANKENSTEIN

Master - master - not mean kill. Master - not hate you! Woman - no woman for Frankenstein - Alone --
> (Beating breast)

Alone.
> (WALDMAN has risen, standing before
> Victor and Amelia. FRANKENSTEIN get
> up, goes to him -- raises arms menacingly.
> WALDMAN stands perfectly calm, facing
> him)
> (Astonished)

You.. not fear --You..man --Frankenstein kill. Hate all men. Master dead.. You..
> (Again raises arms - WALDMAN remains
> calm, crucifix in hand)

Men fear death .. I am death.

WALDMAN

Kill me, if it is God's will. I am not afraid.
> (Bows head over crucifix, clasped in hands)

FRANKENSTEIN

What - that? I saw -- like that --in hut. Man hang on wall.

WALDMAN

That is the son of God. He was killed - by man who hated him. He died to save all men from death.

FRANKENSTEIN

All men. I not man.

WALDMAN

I don't know what you are. When you killed Katrina you felt pain.

FRANKENSTEIN

Yes, pain - pain. Why he not tell me shining water kill? Love Katrina - not like that -- love --
> (Points towards Amelia)

WALDMAN

Pain - that kind of pain is not felt by animals, it comes from the soul. Even when you killed him, you felt pain --
> (Points to window)

But you - I do not understand.

                        FRANKENSTEIN
Soul - what is soul?

                         WALDMAN
It is a part of God. He gives it to every man who lives. After
man dies God calls it back to himself.
           (FRANKENSTEIN murmurs: "not man.")
That's why I'm not afraid to die. You can kill my body, but
not my soul. Katrina is with God; I think that after all he has
suffered, Henry's spirit is with God too.

                        FRANKENSTEIN
Where is God? I thought he -
          (Points to window)
God - my God.

                         WALDMAN
          (Holds crucifix up)
No - God is there. Here - everywhere.

                        FRANKENSTEIN
Your God, yes - - Your God hates me.

                         WALDMAN
God loves the birds, the beasts, as well as men.

                        FRANKENSTEIN
Love - love Frankenstein?

                         WALDMAN
Yes. Whatever you are, you have taught me, a priest, something
about God. He loves you.

                        FRANKENSTEIN
You - you know - that?

                         WALDMAN
He has allowed you to feel pain, and sorrow. He has caused you
to repent - -

                        FRANKENSTEIN
No - friend?

                         WALDMAN
Yes.

                        FRANKENSTEIN
show - -way to Him. Not want .. kill .. more.

          (LIGHTENING - spark goes through machine)

                         WALDMAN
I cannot do that. I can only tell you - that you must ask Him
yourself. You have seen men pray. Ask his forgiveness for your
murders.

                        FRANKENSTEIN
Men hate me.

(LOUDER THUNDER)

WALDMAN
Katrina did not hate you. You killed Katrina.

FRANKENSTEIN
(Suddenly sobs loudly, backs toward window, holds up hands)
Katrina .. Friend .. God!
(Stretches up arms)
God - God help me.
(He falls back into the partly wreaked machine. Instantly a great flash of lightning and a crash of thunder. It seems to strike the hut. The machine hisses, etc. as in Act One, gives off queer colored lights. Lamp goes out. Darkness but for bazier. AMELIA screams WALDMAN drags Frankenstein's body so the face is near bazier. He has a look of peace.)

WALDMAN
(In awe)
There was no other way. The machine that brought him to life has killed him. This was God's answer - His voice was in the thunderbolt.

AMELIA
Victor. Take me away, take me away. Victor, don't leave me. Don't ever leave me.
(They go out)

(WALDMAN lays cross on breast of Frankenstein, looks at him a moment and then slowly follows them)

C U R T A I N

www.ingramcontent.com/pod-product-compliance
Lightning Source LLC
Chambersburg PA
CBHW081258170426
43198CB00017B/2830